CAN
CITIES
SURVIVE?

The Fiscal Plight

of American

Cities

CAN
CITIES
SURVIVE?

The Fiscal Plight

of American

Cities

Robert B. Pettengill

Jogindar S. Uppal

St. Martin's Press   New York

Library of Congress Catalog Card Number: 72-95903
Copyright © 1974 by St. Martin's Press, Inc.
All Rights Reserved.
Manufactured in the United States of America.
For information, write: St. Martin's Press, Inc.,
175 Fifth Avenue, New York, N.Y. 10010

AFFILIATED PUBLISHERS: Macmillan Limited, London—
also at Bombay, Calcutta, Madras, and Melbourne.

PREFACE

Someone has defined an economic problem as an economic situation many influential people don't like and want to do something about. A host of urban difficulties would fit this definition. Public and private leaders loudly deplore inadequate schools, poor transportation, excessive or insufficient welfare payments, crime in the streets, air and water pollution, and the like. Moreover, the demands placed on city governments are continually rising. City employees are as vociferous as those in private enterprise in their demands for higher pay. City dwellers want more and more done for them by their governments, and at the same time they protest having to pay the bills for the added or improved services. All seem unable to understand why economic progress, which has been our salvation in the past, now fails us.

Conflict is inevitable in a world of scarcity, but paralyzing bitterness and violent confrontations are not. Of course each rival faction in our cities wants a bigger share of the urban resource pie, wants to get more and contribute less; but it should be possible to reach nonviolent solutions to most of the economic problems that now divide us. Though the actual pie cutting at any given moment is influenced greatly by how the pie has been divided in the past, there are times when economic changes force new appraisals of relative need and relative power. At these times, if enough people understand the fiscal facts of urban life, workable compromises can be reached. It is the goal of this book to foster the understanding that makes such solutions possible.

Consider, for instance, the revenue-sharing proposals of the past few years. City dwellers declare a temporary truce in their battles over city budgets and unite in a demand that "the state" or "the nation" pay some of their bills. But they rarely seem to realize that the revenue to be "shared" comes from the whole taxpaying public of which they are a part. Few try to calculate whether their city's income from revenue sharing will be greater or less than the consequent increase in the state or federal taxes which they have to pay. An understanding of economic reality would help these people considerably in their search for a genuine solution to their problems.

Another example of the need for fiscal insight is the frequent complaint by some citizens that they are forced to pay for public benefits, such as welfare, that other people receive. When payers and receivers are separated by wide economic and social differences, as in our large cities, it becomes difficult for each side to understand the position of the other. A bit of analysis will show, however, that the receivers of city funds are also direct or indirect taxpayers in more ways than are generally recognized, and the complaining payers are also receivers in ways of which they themselves may be unaware.

In this book the authors present and analyze data that are relevant to these and other major economic problems of American cities. As our footnotes indicate, we have drawn upon the work of numerous experts whose careful research has revealed cause-and-effect relationships among urban variables. We have used the most recent available statistics, generally those from the 1970 Census. Yet this book is not meant to be an econometric research monograph or a theoretical treatise aimed at erudite scholars. Rather, it is intended to promote better understanding of urban fiscal problems among college students, general readers, and, we hope, influential decision makers, both public and private.

Writing as political economists, we have consciously made some value judgments. We like some economic policies better than others, but we realize the frequent necessity for choosing the second best in a world of many constraints. Political power is as much a fact of urban life as scarcity of resources. Decisions about city budgets are chiefly political ones, departing somewhat from those that would emerge from a careful balancing of desires in the marketplace. We dare to hope that one result of our efforts will be a fuller realization of the interdependence of economics and politics.

And now acknowledgments. First, we are grateful to our wives, who have graciously endured our absence as our work proceeded. Second, we thank the reviewers and editorial staff of St. Martin's Press, who made many useful criticisms of the style and substance of the manuscript. Finally, we are especially indebted to Donald Walsh of the New York State Conference of Mayors and Village Officials for his continuing advice and encouragement.

ROBERT B. PETTENGILL

JOGINDAR S. UPPAL

Albany, New York

CONTENTS

1

DEFINING THE

PROBLEM

Cities and Survival

When people ask "Can cities survive?" what might they mean? In what ways could the question make sense? How much of it is scare-mongering? How much is political; how much economic? No final answers can be given to questions like these, but the possibilities should certainly be explored. This requires much statistical research as later chapters will show. At the beginning, however, it is the conceptual framework that needs to be analyzed.

The first task is that of definition. One concept of "city" is that of a large group of people living and working in a small area described in a state charter.[1] If "survival" means "continuing to exist," then in this demographic and political sense it is safe to predict, not only that cities will survive for some time to come, but that they will grow larger and that there will be more of them. If there are today 153 cities in the United States with more than 100,000 people, in another thirty years there will be twice that number.

Viewing cities as concentrations of industrial, commercial, and residential buildings, we may also predict survival. Barring nuclear war, with "second strike" and "third strike" action by major powers in which enemy cities become smoldering targets, cities as people and cities as buildings are here to stay. Natural disasters and man-made holocausts may destroy cities temporarily, but they are likely to be rebuilt on the ruins like many an ancient city. Compared with these destructive forces, economic and political difficulties seem puny indeed, yet in the short run in which we live they may constitute real crises.

To some observers mere survival, mere existence, is not enough. Growth is a key value in contemporary American culture. That is why some people, like Jane Jacobs, think of a static city or one losing population or industry as dead or dying in a metaphorical sense.[2] A healthy city is deemed one where there is a continuing rise in both population and per capita income or wealth. Yet city charters, once given by a state, are not revoked for either demographic or economic reasons, though some of a city's delegated powers may be temporarily suspended for fiscal malfeasance. Sometimes a certain population is needed to qualify for various benefits, political or economic, and these are denied to cities below that critical size.

Looking at City Fiscal Problems

The economic problems of cities depend on who is doing the appraising and what criteria they are applying at the time they make the value judgment. This is fundamental. If an economic problem is seen as an economic condition we don't like and want to improve, who are "we" and what are our goals? The "we" who complain may be the mayor and his council, the owners of business firms, workers in these firms, civil service employees, owners of residential property, slum dwellers, those on welfare, taxpayers, creditors, or any other group that looks to the city government for help or protection. Even academic economists may gather at the pantheistic wailing wall, if they identify their gods.

Typical of one concept of the crisis of cities is the taxpayer's lament, "My taxes are killing me!" His complaint is personal and metaphorical, but it is intimately related to our initial question restated, "Can cities survive high taxes?" Both the complaint and the question need analysis.

"High taxes" are as much a state of mind as an objective fact.

Residents of cities where per capita taxes are relatively low on a national scale are almost as apt to complain about the taxes they pay as are residents of other cities taxed more heavily. "Low " and "high" are relative terms. Taxes that are objectively low as compared with those elsewhere are usually subjectively high as compared with what people would rather pay. It seems unlikely that cities or any other governments will ever solve the subjective tax problem by making the majority of taxpayers content with their tax bills. If the weather is good, what else is there to gripe about?

Elected officials are particularly conscious of the extent and vigor of tax complaints. Subjective reactions become translated into objective behavior. Some of this behavior is just talk, but talk influences votes, and votes influence government action. So our question becomes transformed into one of political survival, "What can or should city officials do to get re-elected?" Try to reduce taxpayer complaints or to win in spite of them?

To explore this question thoroughly would take us too far afield, but in this day of expensive political campaigning the economics of winning powerful taxpayer support and defusing homeowner anger cannot be ignored. On the other side of the picture are those whose demands can be satisfied only by tax revenues painfully wrung from business firms and individuals. Political survival requires placating them, the beneficiaries of city spending that is never large enough, not to mention the creditors who have supplied goods or funds in the past and relentlessly demand payment. Urban economics is inextricably entwined with sociology, psychology, law, and politics.

On Solutions

There is another fundamental concept here. Economic problems, like most other problems, are rarely "solved" in the sense of being ended. We merely reduce the gap between desire and achievement. The plight of cities is a tension between a perceived objective state and felt subjective goals. Whatever can be done to bring these closer together helps to solve city problems, fiscal and otherwise. An observed reduction in taxes or in short-term debt, or even a halt to their rise, is an objective achievement, assuming these are perceived as evils to be reduced.

From the subjective side, tensions may be lessened if the people of a city find out that others are much worse off than they are, or if they can be led to focus more on what they get for their taxes and less on the size of the bill. Indirect benefits are harder to perceive than direct. City services often are not appreciated until they fail, as when rubbish remains uncollected in the streets, water pressure falls, or traffic signals falter and one gets rammed by a careless driver. Nearly everyone has deficient historical perspective and will not admit that some things have improved unless confronted again and again by the facts. Some problems are objectively insoluble, or virtually so, like those of some big taxpayers who deplore and want to stop the secular upward trend of government costs in their cities. Yet these problems may find partial subjective solutions.

Objective solutions are also possible in some instances, or at least for some city dwellers. "We" who deplore high property taxes may get some relief by persuading cities to reduce the pressure on us by adopting other forms of taxation like sales taxes or income taxes. Our economic problems may then be solved at the expense of some other taxpayers less vocal or less well organized than ourselves. The gaps between goals and achievement at the city level may also be narrowed by securing additional state or federal aid to increase welfare payments, improve certain community services, or restrain or reduce local taxes. This again involves partially shifting the tax burden elsewhere, even though most city residents do not realize that they themselves must contribute their part of the increase in state or federal taxes which have to be collected to pay for the subsidies to city governments.

Some Political Aspects

Revenue deficiencies are not the only economic problems that cities face, even though they are the only ones that may lead to default on municipal obligations.[3] Contests between rival claimants may seriously divide a city and may lead to election overturns of criticized administrations, but cities survive. Firemen may insist on as much pay as policemen, garbage collectors strike for higher wages and fringe benefits, welfare clients ask for less parsimonious subsistence, parents for less crowded classrooms, and everyone for cleaner, safer streets. As each demand peaks, a fiscal "crisis" appears, because more to one group means less to another, either on the receiving or the paying side. The needless cries for "More!" become an antiphonic chorus with discord replacing harmony.

Some cities are so poorly organized that one wonders how they continue to operate. A few of the smaller cities never had competent leadership in office, never set up adequate accounting systems and budgetary practices. This was partly the fault of the states, which granted their charters without appropriate stipulations, safeguards, and continuing counsel. The inefficient operation of some large cities has been the result of politics more than anything else, mayors versus city councils, elected officials versus professional civil service employees, trying to please competing pressure groups to get votes needed for election or reelection. Many of these aspects of viability have had to be slighted in this volume with its emphasis on economic factors, but they must not be forgotten.

Having shown the different senses in which cities may "survive" and the multiple facets of their fiscal problems in a general way, we can now proceed to a more detailed examination of the causes of their difficulties and the possible ways of securing some amelioration. Chapter 2 presents a historical and cross-sectional review of the expenditure problems of cities. The same approach is used in Chapter 3 with regard to urban revenues. In both chapters the causes of variations are examined with emphasis on differences in city size, age, and region. Unless otherwise indicated by quotations from earlier writers, our figures have been taken or computed from federal government sources, especially those based on the 1970 Census. A fourth chapter examines in some detail the relationships between central cities and their suburbs, focusing chiefly on the 37 largest Standard Metropolitan Statistical Areas. In conclusion, Chapter 5 brings together the threads of fiscal analysis to furnish a basis for evaluating the various proposals that have been made to alleviate the fiscal troubles of our cities and enable them to survive with less financial distress than now prevails.

Throughout these five chapters, the emphasis is on specific fiscal problems of cities and possible solutions using generally a non-technical interdisciplinary approach. The extensive bibliography at the end contains references to scholarly research for those who are interested in more technical and mathematical approaches.

Notes

1 For the U.S. Census Bureau's definition of cities and other forms of local governments, see Chapter 2, p. 12.

2 Jane Jacobs, *The Economy of Cities* (New York: Random House, 1969).

3 For illustrations, see George H. Hempel, *The Postwar Quality of State and Local Bonds* (New York: 1971), National Bureau of Economic Research, pp. 19-39.

2

CITY

EXPENDITURES

Our cities are in a double bind. Expenditures keep going up inexorably while tax revenues lag. One could begin a study of the fiscal plight of cities from either viewpoint, but custom and logic favor putting expenditures first. In the budgetary process attention is directed to the spending side before the question of potential revenues is taken up. Also, in our legislatures appropriation bills precede revenue bills. Therefore, this chapter is devoted to the rises in demand and costs that generate rising expenditures, while consideration of methods and problems of getting additional funds follows in Chapter 3.

Consider the testimony of the mayors of 12 of our major cities before the House Ways and Means Committee on June 11, 1971, when it was considering the topic of general revenue sharing. The group spoke for the Legislative Action Committee of the U.S. Conference of Mayors, a body that includes more than 500 mayors of cities in this country. These men wrestle with city budget problems continually and know whereof they speak.[1] Their diagnosis is similar to that of urban economists, although the emphases differ somewhat.

Mayor Lindsay of New York led off with the statement that:

Over the last couple of decades, our cities have become the guardians of the country's unwanted stepchildren. We have inherited the Nation's problems of poverty, race, and class

7

conflict, physical deterioration, drug addition, archaic public education systems, pollution. Over the last two decades, the chief problems of the country have grown and festered in these cities, and we are the ones who have been asked to find the solutions.

. . . After fixed costs of pensions and debt service, almost 90 percent of our city tax levy goes into six basic areas: welfare education, health services, police, fire and sanitation.

Mayor Gibson of Newark stressed the high unemployment rate of his city, double the national average, and the 30 percent of its people on public assistance. Mayor Alioto of San Francisco pointed out that "over the past ten years more and better public services have been demanded everywhere: more children to be educated, a greater dependence on public welfare, more traffic on streets and highways." He pointed out how cities increasingly have been forced to take over and subsidize the mass transportation function that used to be handled by private enterprise. Taking another approach, he said that "inflation is the greatest cause of increased city expenditures during recent years." Its impact has been greater in some areas, like education, than in others. "In only two functional areas, public welfare and general administration, did change in scope or quality of services outweigh inflation." Wage rates, he said, have gone up faster for city employees than for those in most other types of employment.

Mayor Maier of Milwaukee told of a computer analysis of his city's budgets, which shows that the city has had "an increase in the young, poor, and the aged" leading to increased "demands for health, police, fire, education and for recreational services."

Several mayors spoke of having been forced to reduce services, not of trying to increase them. The reductions included cuts in the number of city employees, including firemen, policemen, and teachers, not to mention office workers and minor officials. There are very few new programs, new facilities, and new efforts to improve the quality of life in cities. Little or no money is available to pay for hunting for new approaches to fiscal problems. Costs of old programs and maintaining old facilities (the older, the costlier to maintain) have risen faster than available revenues from existing taxes. Yet certain problems are clearly new, such as drug addiction and pollution. The costs of dealing with crime, caring for the elderly, and disposing of solid wastes have increased frighteningly. Cities must spend more per addict, more per criminal, if they hope to reduce these plagues, yet they cannot seem to find enough money even to maintain traditional services at present levels.

The mayor of Detroit, like several others, emphasized the national policies that have led to mass migrations of rural poor into the cities and have raised prices and unemployment rates. He pointed out that managing a big city is like managing a big business and argued that allegations of relative inefficiency in the administrations of cities are generally not true.

In Baltimore, in five years, the education budget has doubled, and police costs have risen 80 percent. Yet its tax base has remained small. Many other cities are similar havens of the poor and likewise short on people with tax-paying ability.

Some Measures of Budget Increases During the Sixties

Some idea of the magnitude of spending increases during the fifties and sixties can be obtained from the Table 2.1, which compares federal, state, and local figures, with a column added for cities alone.

TABLE 2.1

**Percentage Increase in Total Government
Expenditures Per Capita, 1950–70**

	Federal	State	Local	Cities
1950–60	83%	65%	92%	103%
1960–70	90	122	82	104

NOTE: For definition of "cities" in the *U.S. Census of Governments,* see explanation below in this chapter.

SOURCE: Computed from Tax Foundation, *Facts and Figures on Government Finance* (New York, 1960–61 and 1970).

TABLE 2.2

Total Spending Per Capita for U.S. Cities by Population Size, 1971–72
(In descending order of totals for all cities)

Function	All Cities	1 Million or More (6)	500,000– 999,999 (21)	300,000– 499,999 (21)	200,000– 299,999 (17)	100,000– 199,999 (88)	50,000– 99,999 (231)	Below 50,000 (17,663)
Education	$ 38.94	$110.91	$ 46.19	$ 53.58	$ 50.46	$ 45.47	$ 32.58	$ 12.11
Police	29.86	64.57	42.50	31.29	30.19	27.25	23.54	18.02
Welfare	22.96	120.43	38.08	6.17	8.43	5.70	2.95	0.86
Fire protection	16.73	27.00	22.92	22.06	22.97	21.36	18.63	9.43
Hospitals	14.66	53.17	24.61	6.46	5.56	6.94	6.00	5.84
Highways	12.20	11.20	11.45	9.97	11.31	11.60	12.03	13.24
Parks and recreation	11.90	13.21	21.28	20.56	18.52	15.71	13.28	6.58
Interest on debt	11.57	24.73	15.30	15.55	14.44	11.13	8.41	6.75
Sanitation	10.11	19.47	13.24	10.81	13.39	10.63	8.65	6.38
Sewerage	5.60	3.91	8.03	8.05	6.16	5.95	5.36	5.22
Health	5.18	19.60	11.09	4.69	3.78	2.91	2.02	0.74
Housing	4.36	15.01	7.03	5.24	5.93	4.36	2.32	0.71
All functions	220.90	549.71	322.45	228.08	233.76	201.79	165.38	110.77

NOTE: The figures on total spending per capita exclude capital outlays. The number of cities in each size group is given in parenthesis.

SOURCE: U.S. Bureau of the Census, *City Government Finances, 1971–72.*

City spending clearly rose the fastest, though it was surpassed by the rate of growth in state spending in the second decade. The doubling of spending in both the fifties and the sixties indicates the probable magnitude of city fiscal problems in the seventies. If inflation proves to be worse than in the two previous decades, budgetary difficulties will be that much greater.

During the same period, the gross national product (GNP) rose slightly less rapidly than the total of government expenditures. Therefore, public spending took a larger fraction of total income in 1970 than in 1960. For all governments, the percentage rose about one-seventh, from 27 percent of GNP to 31 percent. For cities the rise occurred at substantially the same rate, from 3.02 percent of GNP to 3.51 percent. Since the property tax base used by most cities for the major portion of their income does not rise as rapidly as the GNP,[2] this rise in spending was made possible only by special efforts, which will be described in following chapters.

Some cities suffered more from their financial pinch than did others. The very largest, those with populations in excess of one million, experienced the greatest budgetary demands, as shown by Table 2.2. Between 1960 and 1971, per capita spending for all functions in this group rose 269 percent. In the 500,000-1 million group, spending rose only 189 percent; and in the smallest size group, cities below 50,000, the per capita increase was only 110 percent (see Table 2.3, p. 18). However, studies to be cited later contain evidence that other factors are more important than mere size. Furthermore, most of the very large cities are in the North Central and Northeastern states, which have problems (e.g., greater traffic congestion, population density) different from somewhat smaller and newer cities in the South and West.

Some Cautions About Municipal Statistics

In using municipal statistics for intercity or intertemporal comparison, much caution should be exercised because there are so many differences among cities both currently and historically. Chief among these are overlapping jurisdictions, peculiar state definitions, functions performed, and accounting methods. For example, two major governmental functions performed for city residents, education and welfare, are financed differently in different cities. In most places schools are administered by officials of special school districts, which raise revenues by property taxation and get financial help from the state government. In nine cities over 300,000, however, the public schools in 1969-70 were operated by the cities themselves rather than by an independent school district. This raised the total per capita spending of those cities and made them appear to be more expensive places to live than other cities, where school budgets were separate. Since school spending has risen more rapidly than many other governmental functions, this budgetary peculiarity would also help to explain why the rates of increase in total per capita spending have been higher in the aggregates of the size groups to which these cities belong.

Similarly, the counties usually take care of welfare spending, another big item in modern governmental budgets. City budgets are correspondingly reduced, even though most of the welfare spending goes to city residents. However, there are exceptions. Fourteen of the largest cities, including 12 of the 27 with 500,000 to 1 million inhabitants, are, in effect, composite city-county governments and absorb in their budgets not only welfare costs but all other county functions, such as health, highways, and law enforcement. Again, we note the statistical incomparability element both as between individual cities and as between city aggregates grouped by size.

According to the Census,[3] local governments are of five types: counties, municipalities, townships, school districts, and special districts (e.g., sewer districts). When the word "city" is used, it refers to all those municipalities (total 18,048) popularly known as cities, villages that have a municipal form of government, and towns in 42 states (all states except New York, Wisconsin, and the 6 New England states). Townships are a legal entity in the above 8 states plus 12 more in the Midwest. In New York State, there are such anomalies as the town of Hempstead not being counted as a city even though it has about 800,000 population, whereas small places like Little Falls and Salamanca, with populations of less than 9,000, are included in Census data as "cities."

Another caution should be advanced against thinking of cities as a relatively homogeneous group so far as their fiscal problems are concerned. Some have peculiar revenue-raising problems. Others differ in their expenditure patterns. For instance, following Brazer, we find that in 1948 the highest per capita expenditures for the combined common functions and also for police and fire protection separately were in resort cities, followed by core cities of major metropolitan areas, industrial suburb cities, high income residential suburbs, core cities of minor metropolitan areas, and independent cities.[4]

The resort group was made up of five cities: Miami Beach, Daytona Beach, Fort Lauderdale, Atlantic City, and Reno, each having hotel receipts in 1948 of more than $60.00 per capita. Brazer's analysis showed that the per capita expenditures for common functions in major resort cities were more than twice those in the independent cities (those not located in a Standard Metropolitan Statistical Area). The resort cities also led all others with respect to spending on highways, recreation, general control, and sanitation, but there was no regular pattern of ranking among the other city types for these last four expenditure categories.[5]

The logic of this rank order may be found in its connection with some of the major independent variables to be discussed later, ratio of core city population to fringe population, median income, population density, and percentage of population employed.

There are some other incongruities in municipal data, at least three of which should be mentioned. Total spending, as will be explained below, is a function partly of state aid received and also of federal aid, although most of that is funneled through state treasuries. Whenever aid is on a categorical or qualification basis (the aged, school enrollment, etc.), city characteristics change city budgets. For instance, if welfare aid is related to the number of families with incomes below $3,000, obviously cities with a high percentage of poor people get more aid and spend more in that category than cities of the same size that are more affluent.

Capital expenditures are sometimes included in the reported total for an expenditure category, sometimes excluded. Prominent among these are highways, schools, sewage, and housing expenditures. Similarly, welfare spending includes both cash transfers and the costs of running the program. Recent tabulations, like 1964-65, separate these; earlier ones such as 1960 did not.

Cities differ in their accounting procedures and may even change these from one city administration to another for fancied political advantage. The handling of capital expense is a case in point. Pazour points out that New York City does not include the amortization of transit equipment in reported costs (and deficits) of its public transportation operations.[6] For large cities like New York, the total involved may be so great as to skew the comparisons between a group containing them and other groups of smaller cities.

Finally, a comment is in order about statistical methods. Most econometric studies of differences in per capita city spending by categories are cross-sectional, not intertemporal; they are static, rather than dynamic. They may give some indication as to why spending for some function has been larger in some cities than in others, but this does not furnish a valid basis for predicting the results of future changes. Useful elasticity functions show how changes in independent variables (population, incomes, etc.) change dependent variables (per capita spending on police and fire protection, sanitation, etc.). The cross-sectional studies based on 1957 data, or 1962, or any other year, merely show how one level of spending in cities of a certain class was associated with one or more characteristics of those cities.[7] Furthermore, the unexplained variations are quite large. Due to the paucity of good time-series comparisons, however, static correlations often have been used to predict what would happen if cities planned for and executed changes in the name of fiscal reform. Such an approach is risky.[8] These and other statistical problems will be pointed out wherever necessary as the analysis proceeds.

Increase in Spending by Cities As a Whole During the Sixties

During the 1960's, the general operating expenditures of U. S. cities nearly tripled, creating severe pressure upon those responsible for raising the revenues needed. As we look ahead we should know what caused the fiscal troubles of the past. How much was unavoidable? How much was the result of poor planning or execution?

At least one major cause of the increase was beyond the control of the cities themselves—the 50 percent nationwide rise in the prices of goods and services. True, the cities could have fought harder against attempts by city employees to get wage increases, a major cause of fiscal migraine, but the general upward trend of wages and prices derived from the nation's social, fiscal, and monetary policies could not be denied.

Nor could cities have done much about the 2 percent rise in city population during the decade. This is less than the 8 percent presumptive natural increase (national average) of their own residents during the decade. The net increase in spite of substantial white emigration was the result of significant immigration from less prosperous regions, particularly the rural South, but also from Puerto Rico, Cuba, and other foreign countries.

For some cities, particularly the large ones and those on the Atlantic Coast, ships, planes, buses, and cars brought more new fiscal problems than did the stork. While noting this fact, one should not lose sight of the offsetting contribution that immigrants made to the income and the tax-paying capacities of the cities to which they came.[9]

An additional cause of growth in urban spending was the demand of city people for more and better services. Some single out the demand for more aid to the poor as the major cause of unbalanced budgets. This complaint of the more affluent has some element of truth in it. If city fathers, for political or humanitarian reasons, decide to raise welfare budgets closer to the Social Security Administration (SSA) poverty line (it is rarely exceeded), that costs money.[10] High welfare payments also attract people from regions where the political powers are less generous or less responsive to the wishes of the poor. But this is a minor cause of urban fiscal distress because direct and indirect federal and state aid in this field is so extensive. According to a recent paper[11] in 1969 the federal government financed 58 percent of welfare aid, the states 30 percent, and local government only 12 percent for the country as a whole. The 48 largest cities spent $2.8 billion on public welfare during 1971-72. State aid for this function came to $2.3 billion (i.e., 82 percent of city expenditure in this category). Figures on total federal aid to cities for welfare are difficult to compute since most of it either goes directly to recipients or is channeled through states.

There has also been a demand for better police protection. Crime on city streets has alarmed residents to the point of making them willing to pay for more police patrols, even though some students of city problems believe that this is a very expensive method and one that does not get at the roots of the problem. An alternative remedy, economic and social diversification in residential areas, might possibly reduce crime but would be difficult to implement.

Other services for which there has been a rising demand are better schools and highways, better health care for the poor, better fire protection for all. In nearly every case, this has meant higher per capita spending, even above and beyond the effects of inflation. Whether the increased spending thus figured has brought a wide-spread rise in the quality and quantity of city services could be answered only by a careful examination of each expenditure category and the establishment of acceptable norms. In any case, the increased urban expenditures that are one side of the urban crisis are clearly the result of rising demand as well as rising unit costs, and that demand continues to rise. It follows, first, that cities in trouble cannot blame their fiscal difficulties entirely on outside forces and, second, that the remedies lie partly within. The fat man who eats too much may blame his genes but also must confess his lack of will power.

A less obvious explanation of some of the increased cost of city government can be found in the cities' assumption of services formerly performed by private enterprise, notably transportation. This does not show in any of the common function categories usually mentioned, but public transportation deficits are becoming larger and larger by the year. New York City is a notorious example. Among other cases of public assumption of private functions, one must note: the substitution of public schools for parochial schools; the increased use of public higher education (community colleges) in place of private higher education; the lifting of some of the welfare assistance load from private philanthropy; the increased provisions for hospital care for indigents; and the substitution of public for private housing.

John Pazour has summarized the relative impact of these expenditure-increasing forces as follows:

> For all general expenditures in the fifteen years between 1955 and 1969, inflation accounted for well over forty percent of the total increase in outlays. Only one fourth was due to workload, and less than one third was accounted for by changes in scope or quality of services. The impact of inflation also varied among different municipal functions. Higher prices had the most noticeable effect upon local schools and basic urban services [but] . . . was below average in the case of public welfare, higher education, and general administration.[12]

The costs of urban government have risen more rapidly than those of most private industry because of the limited opportunities for substituting capital equipment in the types of service jobs where most government employees function (police, firemen, teachers, office clerks, etc.). Rising productivity in manufacturing offsets part of the wage increases forced by inflation and collective bargaining. To recruit and retain employees, government wage scales must rise in keeping with those in private industry, but without most of the offsetting economies that the profit motive and mechanization provide.[13] Some computerization of office work is thus far the only area where appreciable productivity gains can be achieved in government matching those outside.

Some Changes in Spending by City Size Groups and by Categories

For the largest cities the biggest budget items, welfare and education, are also the items that had the greatest rate of increase between 1960 and 1972.[14] This is shown in Table 2.3. Welfare expenditures per capita went up 579 percent; educational expenditures per capita went up 313 percent. Police and hospital costs rose

TABLE 2.3

Increase in Per Capita Total Spending for U.S. Cities, by Population Size, 1960–72
(In descending order of percentage increase for all cities)

Function	All Cities	1 Million or More	500,000–999,999	300,000–499,999	200,000–299,999	100,000–199,999	50,000–99,999	Below 50,000
Welfare	338.2%	579.2%	271.1%	40.9%	229.3%	45.8%	—	—
Housing and urban renewal	285.8	204.7	490.8	389.7	872.1	581.2	452.4%	273.7%
Health	272.7	534.3	290.5	159.1	111.2	92.7	83.6	34.5
Interest on debt	211.9	170.6	235.6	297.2	188.0	245.6	187.0	216.9
Hospitals	199.8	290.1	187.2	85.1	20.6	32.7	100.0	141.3
Education	197.7	312.8	188.9	280.3	196.8	176.2	115.6	47.1
Sewerage	175.9	138.4	211.2	283.3	133.3	162.1	144.7	155.9
Police	171.7	211.9	155.7	160.1	161.4	150.5	141.9	147.8
Parks and recreation	150.5	96.3	186.8	169.1	215.5	141.1	154.9	88.0
Fire protection	119.3	175.5	110.3	126.7	135.8	113.8	106.1	62.9
Highways	113.5	48.3	81.7	84.6	86.0	76.02	82.3	80.1
Sanitation	108.4	108.7	106.9	104.3	113.2	106.8	83.6	100.0
All functions	181.2	269.3	189.3	183.5	176.1	141.8	116.0	110.5

NOTE: The expenditures on capital outlays are not included in the figures on per capita spending. For the year 1960, per capita expenditure for cities with populations below 50,000 has been computed by averaging expenditures for cities with population sizes 25,000–50,000 and below 25,000.

SOURCE: U.S. Bureau of the Census, City Government Finances, 1960 and 1971–72.

212 and 290 percent, respectively. These last two costs become more prominent in the budgets of smaller (below 50,000) cities, where, as explained above, welfare costs are rarely included. If relatively small items are included in the ranking, the increase in health spending would have to be accorded second place (534 percent), but its total in 1972 was way down in seventh spot, only $19.60 per capita, as compared to $110.91 for education.

The pattern for medium-sized cities appears quite different. The biggest items in the budgets for cities of 300,000-500,000 inhabitants in 1972 were education ($53.58 per capita), police protection ($31.29), fire protection ($22.06), parks and recreation ($20.56). Among the major items, education remains at the top in terms of percentage increase (280 percent). Three small items, however, had even greater percentage increases, housing (390 percent), interest on debt (297 percent), and sewerage (283 percent).

Examining the very smallest cities, those with less than 50,000 inhabitants, we find that education drops to third in total spending—due, no doubt, to separate school district financing of nearly all educational activities. Note the decline from the large city's $110.91 per capita to the small city's $12.11 per capita, which obviously does not signify a decrease in per pupil spending by that amount nor any such decrease in the quality of education offered to children of the smaller cities. In this group of small cities the leading budget item is for police protection ($18.02), followed by highways ($13.24). However, for rate of increase, the police percentage rank is only fourth and highways eighth, both trailing housing, interest on debt, and sewerage.

For most cities, among major items, education is at the top both in cost per capita and in percentage of increase. City welfare burdens are not significant below the 500,000 city-size level because they are borne mostly by county budgets. Police costs are a major budget item for all sizes of city, as are the costs of fire protection. As cities decrease in size, the costs of highway maintenance rise as a fraction of the budget, while hospital costs decline (again, most likely because of county financing). Sanitation costs per capita fall in amount but rise as percentage of total budgets.

The same is true of interest on debt, but its relative position in the increase scale changes markedly. Debt charges rose more rapidly than any other expense except housing in cities with populations of less than 200,000. However, debt charges per capita for small cities are only one-third of those in the very large cities (those with populations over 1 million) and about half those in the middle-sized cities.

Explanations of the High Rates
of Increase in City Per Capita Spending

Returning to the question of probable causes, other than inflation, of the increase in city spending, which has caused so much trouble for those who must find the money to pay for the rising costs, we find a few analytical studies that support in general the mayors' comments that introduced this chapter. Hirsch shows that the main cause has been the rising percentage of the poor and nonwhites in central cities.[15] Between 1960 and 1969, the percentage of the nation's poor (SSA definition) residing in central cities rose from 28 percent to 32 percent, the black population from 16.2 to 21.3 percent. Numerous studies reveal the low educational level of blacks compared with whites and of poor people compared to the more affluent. The disadvantaged would require more educational dollars per pupil if they were to be raised to national norms, a rather improbable achievement given the white, upper and middle class composition of most school boards. Nevertheless, a high percentage of poor nonwhites in cities does raise education costs, as the next section describes.[16]

The connection between poverty and welfare payments does not need elaboration, but again note the previous caution regarding intercity, interstate, and interregional differences in governmental budgeting for welfare expenses. Note also the differing amounts of state and federal aid to different classes of needy persons and the various methods of channeling it to them.

An entirely different cause of rising costs of city government is the rise in wages and salaries paid to city employees. We have no evidence that higher pay rates have been associated with offsetting increases in productivity. The total bill for personal services rose during the sixties most rapidly in the largest cities: 117 percent in those over 1 million, falling to a 77 percent increase in the middle-sized cities and 44 percent in the smallest, all in keeping with what one would expect, since the larger cities are more likely to have strong and aggressive unions of civil service employees. During this interval the total number of municipal employees increased only 36 percent.

One other clear trend has contributed to the fiscal plight of cities by creating pressure on the expenditure side, the growing use of the city streets and facilities by commuters and shoppers.[17] The figures in Table 2.4 show the rise in the percentage of fringe population to that of the core city. City suburbs have been growing faster than cities, but the people who moved there from former homes in the central cities usually continue to work in the city and commute back and forth. They also do some of their shopping in the city, despite the development of suburban shopping plazas. The resulting extra demand for police services and street mainte-nance is a natural one and is borne out by numerous cross-sectional

TABLE 2.4

Population Changes by Types of Residence, 1960–69
(In millions)

Type of Residence	1960 Population	1969 Population	Percentage Change
United States	178.7	200.1	12%
Metropolitan areas	112.4	129.6	15
Central cities	57.8	58.7	2
Suburban rings	54.6	70.9	30
Suburban fringe population as percentage of central city population	94.0%	121.0%	

SOURCE: U.S. Bureau of the Census, *Trends in Social and Economic Condi-tions in Metropolitan and Non-Metropolitan Areas,* Special Studies, No. 33, September 1970, p. 2.

studies, which show high positive correlations between high percentages of contact populations and city operating budgets, particularly for the police category. In a very comprehensive recent study of both static and dynamic relationships, Phillip E. Vincent[18] shows that commuting workers add more to the economy of cities than they impose by way of extra costs but that the urban burdens from suburban shoppers exceed the gains from them.

A number of students of urban problems (Hirsch, Adams, Bahl, etc.) have demonstrated a clear associational correlation between high density of population and high spending per capita for most of the common functions, notably police and fire protection. Thus, the higher spending per capita in larger cities can also be explained on the basis of their greater population density. The relevant figures for the central cities in the 25 largest Standard Metropolitan Statistical Areas in Table 2.5 show that, with some exceptions, larger cities have greater density of population and, hence, higher spending per capita for most city functions. Among the causes of high population density are the age of the city and natural barriers to expansion such as adjacent bodies of water—the oceans, lakes, and major rivers.

Fiscal Impact of Nonwhites in Central Cities

The percentage of nonwhites in central cities rose from 16 percent in 1960 to almost 22 percent in 1970. This resulted from a major influx of blacks compared with a minor immigration of whites (actually a net white exodus), accentuated by a significantly higher birth rate in resident black families. Most of the urban newcomers, who included some immigrants from abroad (especially Puerto Ricans, Cubans, and Mexicans), came from rural areas, where their levels of living were below the average in the cities to which they went. Presumably the migrants chose as their destinations the cities where they had friends or relatives or which already had large settlements of their own kind. Cities on the Mexican border and port cities were therefore most affected by the foreign migration, while North-South "border cities" generally

TABLE 2.5

Population and Density of Population in the Central Cities of 25 Largest SMSA's, 1970

City	Population (in thousands)	Density Per Square Mile
New York	7,868	26,252
Chicago	3,367	15,187
Los Angeles-Long Beach	3,175	6,975
Philadelphia	1,949	15,164
Detroit	1,511	10,953
Houston	1,233	3,841
San Francisco-Oakland	1,077	11,037
Baltimore	906	11,568
Dallas	844	3,324
Indianapolis	792	11,302
Washington, D.C.	757	12,321
Cleveland	751	9,893
St. Paul-Minneapolis	744	7,056
Milwaukee	717	7,986
San Diego	697	3,579
Boston	641	13,936
St. Louis	622	10,167
New Orleans	593	2,891
Seattle-Everett	584	6,353
Phoenix	582	3,103
Columbus	540	6,217
Pittsburgh	520	9,440
Denver	515	7,602
Kansas City	507	3,892
Tampa-St. Petersburg	494	4,056

NOTE: Density per square mile varies considerably among the largest cities because of annexations and accidents of initial boundaries. All of them have congested "downtown" areas, but some are spread out so much that for the entire city, the statistical density per square mile is relatively low.

SOURCE: U.S. Bureau of the Census, *Statistical Abstract of the United States*, 1972, pp. 837–80.

serve as way stations for blacks en route from the South to large
cities farther north.

It is an axiom of much urban fiscal literature that the increasing
percentage of blacks in our central cities creates budget problems,
that they increase expenditures far more than they increase revenues. Just how much and in which categories, however, has not
been altogether clear. Henry S. Terrell has suggested an explanation.[19] He has shown that the main expenditure impact of
the blacks in central cities in 1960 was upon educational expenses.
Although the amount spent per pupil remains unchanged because
of budget discrimination against predominantly black schools,
total school expense is proportionally greater in cities with high
black population because black families have larger numbers of
school-age children and because a higher percentage of blacks is
enrolled in the relatively more expensive vocational training
programs.[20] The unweighted mean impact of nonwhites on educational expenditures in 40 cities with either a dependent school
district or a coterminous independent district was $3.53 per
capita, or $14.12 per family of four.[21] The corresponding impact
on the other side of the budget was to reduce revenues by $3.80 per
capita, for a weighted total educational impact of $6.60 per
person, or about $25.00 per family. This amounts to approxi-
mately half of 1 percent of the median family's income in the 40
cities.

The variation among cities was large, ranging from zero nonwhite expenditure impact in San Jose to $10.46 in Cleveland,
$9.93 in Detroit, and $9.33 in Newark.

In most cities with a high percentage of nonwhites, whites have
a strong racial incentive to send their children to private schools.
This is a major factor in making the ratio of nonwhites to total
enrollment in urban public schools significantly higher than their
ratio to the city population as a whole. See Table 2.6, which gives
the figures for the 10 large cities with the highest percentage of
nonwhites in 1970. All the cities follow the described pattern, and
school costs are higher per student than in white-predominant
schools.

Those who have not studied the data carefully tend to stress the

TABLE 2.6

Population and Enrollment of Nonwhites in Public Schools in 10
Central Cities with Highest Percentage of Blacks
and Other Nonwhite Population, 1970

Central City	Nonwhite Population As Percentage of Total Population	Nonwhite As Percentage of Total Public School Enrollment	
		Below High School	High School
Washington, D.C.	72.3%	90.6%	86.6%
Newark	56.0	75.2	67.6
Augusta, Ga.	50.2	62.1	61.6
Baltimore	47.0	60.1	55.6
New Orleans	45.5	62.2	53.4
Charleston	45.4	58.3	54.0
Wilmington	44.1	65.0	56.7
Richmond	42.4	53.8	51.2
Birmingham	42.2	51.8	51.0
St. Louis	41.3	56.3	50.9

SOURCE: U.S. Bureau of the Census, *Statistical Abstract of the United States*, 1972, pp. 838–97.

growing welfare burden as a major cause of urban fiscal distress and blame it in turn upon the rising percentage of nonwhites. Terrell shows that this is not true for most cities.[22] Only 12.4 percent of the funds expended for the six major public welfare programs in 1963 throughout the United States came from local sources. The highest percentage financed locally was the category of "General Assistance," 49.9 percent, but its total was only 36 percent of all locally financed welfare aid. And since most cities lie in counties that raise some of the needed welfare funds and administer their disbursement, the impact on city budgets is generally very small. For instance, in 1970-1971, Boston spent $11.08 per capita on welfare, but only $5.47 of this amount came from the city budget, while New York City spent $254.04, but raised only $48.24 from its own sources. More important, then, than the question of how much welfare goes to nonwhites is the overall part that welfare plays in the fiscal burdens of our cities. In fact, "the affluent are not able to avoid the bulk of their responsibilities for providing welfare assistance by altering their residence, since the federal government provides over one-half of the funds for assistance payments."[23] Further, moving to the suburbs frequently leaves them in the same county as that of the central city from whose welfare burdens some may think they are escaping.

Terrell's figures show that in 1960 the total adverse impact of nonwhites on city budgets (revenue, education, welfare, and police) had a mean value of $15.61 per capita, ranging from a low of $0.75 in San Jose to $42.60 in Richmond. Twelve of the 46 cities reveal impacts of more than 1 percent of the municipal income per capita. The greatest impact was in the three border cities of Richmond (2.19 percent), Baltimore (1.91 percent), and St. Louis (1.76 percent). Terrell calls these "entrepôt cities," way stations on the route north. He presents figures to show that they "tend to receive the poorest, least educated, and least skilled non-whites, who upon entrance will have a relatively large impact on the public sector. . . . Clearly the entrepôt cities, with their much wider gaps between educational attainment [of immigrants and emigrants], are net exporters of educated non-whites as compared to the terminus cities."[24] From this one may infer that residents of northern cities are deriving a net benefit from expenditures by border cities.

Finally, Terrell shows that the higher the adverse impact of nonwhites on city budgets, the slower the rise in the per capita income levels of those cities, with the result that fiscal problems become more acute. Part of this is due to the emigration of the higher income whites from larger central cities to their suburbs. From 1955 to 1960, for instance, when the percentage of nonwhites was rising, central cities had four times as many white emigrants as white immigrants. One must recognize, however, that color consciousness was not the only reason for white emigration. Also important were rising incomes, improved transportation opportunities, movement of industries to the suburbs, and upper and middle class dislike of the lower class culture patterns of the immigrants, both white and nonwhite.

FACTORS CAUSING RISE IN POLICE EXPENDITURES

Table 2.7 shows for fiscal 1972 a clear correlation between the size of a city and its per capita police spending. (A similar though less strong correlation existed from 1960 to 1972 between city size and *increases* in police expenditures per capita; see Table 2.3.)

TABLE 2.7

Per Capita Police Costs Vary with Size of Cities, 1971–72

Size of City	Per Capita Police Expenditure
Under 50,000	$18.02
50,000–100,000	23.54
100,000–200,000	27.25
200,000–300,000	30.19
300,000–500,000	31.29
500,000–1 million	42.50
1 million and over	64.57

SOURCE: U.S. Bureau of the Census, *City Government Finances, 1971–72.*

The relationship shown in Table 2.7 is a logical one in several respects. The higher incidence of crime in big cities is well known, as is the relation between crime and the poverty syndrome: slum living, high percentage of nonwhites, abnormal unemployment, many urban immigrants not yet adjusted to their new abode, and so on. Moreover, one would presume that population size and density are closely correlated (sprawling Los Angeles being a notable exception), and density has been shown to be a breeder of crime. Adams made a study of the relation in 1957 between population density per square mile in various cities and police expenditures in those cities.[25] These findings are shown in Table 2.8.

The second most important independent variable affecting police expenditures in Adams' study is the presence of transients. More people coming into the cities for brief stays create greater opportunities for street crimes. Their patronizing of hotels, motels, theaters, convention halls, and so on creates other policing

TABLE 2.8

Per Capita Police Costs Vary with Population Density

Population Density Per Square Mile, 1950	Police Expenditures, Adjusted Deviations from Mean, 1957
433–598	− .105
599–930	+ .191
931–1760	+1.378
1761–3420	+1.964
3421–5080	+4.697
5081 and over	+6.492

SOURCE: Robert F. Adams, "On the Variation in the Consumption of Public Services," in Harvey E. Brazer, ed., *Essays in State and Local Finance* (Ann Arbor, Mich.: Institute of Public Administration, University of Michigan, 1967).

difficulties, not to mention traffic problems. A study of the high cost of governing resort cities has already been mentioned. Adams' third factor is a high percentage of the foreign born. Such persons on the whole have difficulties adapting to our cultural patterns, are apt to be poor, suffer from exploitation, and evince other disabilities leading to police expense.

A fourth variable established by Adam's analysis is the percentage of nonwhites in the population. Most people would accept this finding without much question: high crime rates would seem to warrant high police budgets, and blacks commit more crimes per 1,000 persons than whites. The correlation between a high black population and high police expenditure per capita is more true in northern cities than in Southern. In the South, there seems to be a lesser concern for the black victims of black crime. This is a good example of the dangers of using the word "need" as a synonym for "demand." Need is a value-judgment term, the perception of which may differ from culture to culture, while demand has definite economic connotation of the total outlay people are willing to make for a good or service like police protection.

Because of Terrell's[26] disagreement with the commonly ex-

TABLE 2.9

**Crime Rates and Police Expenditures in Cities over 500,000
with Highest Density of Nonwhites, 1970**

City	Percentage of Nonwhites	"Crime Index"	Per Capita Police Expenditure
Washington, D.C.	72.3%	7,835	$114.5
Baltimore	47.0	6,860	63.7
New Orleans	45.5	5,965	26.3
Detroit	44.5	8,447	49.1
St. Louis	41.3	7,382	52.6
Memphis	39.2	3,464	23.4
Cleveland	39.0	5,934	50.8
Chicago	34.4	3,802	55.2
Philadelphia	34.4	2,347	54.8
San Francisco	32.7	7,980	47.1
Houston	26.3	4,857	20.2

SOURCES: U.S. Bureau of the Census, *City Government Finances,* 1970–71; idem, *Statistical Abstract of the United States,* 1972, pp. 836–97; and U.S. Federal Bureau of Investigation, *Uniform Crime Reports for the United States,* 1970, p. 185.

pressed view upheld by Adams, we tried to test the hypothesis by examining 1970 figures as shown in Table 2.9. The first column ranks from high to low 11 major cities of the country in the percentage of nonwhites in the population. The second shows their "crime rates" in terms of a very rough index obtained by a simple addition of figures on the crimes per 100,000 inhabitants reported by the Department of Justice in seven categories for 1970—homicide, rape, robbery, aggravated assault, auto theft, burglary, and larceny.[27] The third column gives per capita police expenditures. Comparing these three columns we find that 6 of the top 7 cities in nonwhite population also fall in the top 7 in "crime index," and 5 of the top 7 in nonwhite population are in the top 7 in per capita police expenditure. Conventional wisdom seems confirmed.

FACTORS CAUSING VARIATIONS
IN FIRE DEPARTMENT EXPENDITURES

The most important of the variables determining the demand for fire protection, and therefore expenditure on it, was found by Adams to be density of population, as might be expected. The most densely populated cities are also the oldest and thus have the oldest, most flammable buildings. This increases the frequency of fires and the costliness of fire fighting equipment. Larger cities also have higher pay scales. The correlation Adams found with transiency of population is reasonable, but that with percentage of foreign born[28] is harder to explain, though it may operate through the age and kind of housing. When we find, however, that there is no correlation with the percentage of nonwhites, the most logical explanation is probably the low political power of blacks in 1957. Even now they rarely own the dilapidated places in which they live and may see the fire departments as a protector more of the landlord than of themselves.

Population Growth May Be a Major Cause of City Fiscal Problems

Does growth in population tend to intensify or alleviate a city's fiscal problems? It depends. If growth is by annexation and the annexed areas have relatively high-income residents and property with high assessed valuation, then the city will find its fiscal troubles reduced. Annexation has been more common than is generally realized. According to the Advisory Commission on Intergovernmental Relations (hereafter ACIR), "It is responsible for nearly all central city population growth since 1950. . . . Without annexation, the 10.8 percent increase in central city population [during the fifties] would drop to 1.5 percent."[29] Cities that have growth without annexation, chiefly those in the South and West, have "had considerable undeveloped land within their own borders, the product of earlier annexations."[30] This is corroborated by the figures for city population increase for 1960-70. With annexation, central cities in the 37 largest Standard Metropolitan Areas grew almost 12.2 percent; without annexation, these central cities would have experienced an actual decline in population.[31]

The decline in population in the larger and older cities of the Northeast and Midwest is well known. It would have been helpful budgetwise only if there had been no attendant decline in the income level of the central city's population and property values per capita did not diminish; but these unfortunate changes did occur. Therefore, even if there were significant, and reversible, diseconomies of scale in the costs of city government with population as the independent variable, the population decline in large cities would not have helped them and probably will not in the future. Figures in Table 2.10 on changes in population and per capita expenditures in the 25 largest cities show that while population has declined in many large cities during the decade 1960-70, their total spending per capita has increased sharply.

Given probable population trends, the urban fiscal future looks bleak. Growth by annexation is likely to be of declining importance in the future, and large cities will probably continue to lose population to their suburbs. Moreover, the density of population will rise in middle-sized and small cities as they grow, and evidence has already been cited to indicate a high correlation between spending per capita and population density. In an early study, Brazer shows this to have been true as far back as 1953 for 462 cities of more than 50,000 people (1950 Census). A smaller sample of the 40 largest cities corroborated the analysis of the larger group:

Again, as in the analysis of the 462 cities, density of population emerges as an important influence upon levels of expenditure. It accounts for a larger proportion of variation in per capita expenditures than any of the other independent variables in the cases of police protection and highways and is also of considerable importance with respect to total general operating expenditures.[32]

The population decreases of the sixties in the larger central cities have not been large enough to offset the budgetary impact of inflation. Further, in cautioning against too facile generalizations,

TABLE 2.10

Percentage Change in Population and Per Capita General Operating Expenditure in 25 Largest Central Cities, 1960–70

Central City	Population Change	Increase in Per Capita Total Expenditure
New York	1.1%	225%
Los Angeles-Long Beach	12.5	87
Chicago	−5.2	125
Philadelphia	−2.7	126
Detroit	−9.5	90
Washington, D.C.	−1.0	238
Boston	−8.1	100
Pittsburgh	−14.0	117
St. Louis	−17.1	118
Baltimore	−3.5	194
Cleveland	−14.3	120
Houston	31.4	69
Newark	−5.6	319
Minneapolis-St. Paul	−6.1	41
Dallas	24.2	64
Seattle-Everett	−4.4	133
Anaheim-Santa Ana-Garden Grove	54.4	158
Milwaukee	−3.3	83
Atlanta	2.0	201
Cincinnati	−9.9	197
Paterson-Clifton-Passaic	1.0	80
San Diego	21.6	98
Buffalo	−13.2	146
Miami	14.8	35
Kansas City	6.7	78

SOURCES: U.S. Bureau of the Census, *General Demographic Trends for Metropolitan Areas, 1960–1970* (Washington, D.C., 1972); and idem, *City Government Finances, 1960–70.*

Brazer makes the important point that America is not homogeneous. Cities of the same rate of increase may differ very much in spending patterns because of differences in age, in state support of governmental functions, in racial composition, in percentage of first generation immigrants, and so forth.[33]

Notes

1 All these quotations from mayors are found in *General Revenue Sharing*, Hearings Before the Committee on Ways and Means, House of Representatives, 92nd Congress, 1st Session, June 11, 1971.

2 Dick Netzer, in his book *Economics of the Property Tax* (Washington, D.C.: Brookings Institution, 1966), gives a 10-city sample indicating an increase in assessed value of property per capita for the period 1957-65 that ranges from an average of 0.25 percent to 3.8 percent per year. During the same period, the per capita GNP rose an average of 4.6 percent per year.

3 U.S. Bureau of the Census, *1970 Census User's Guide*, Part I, p. 79.

4 See Harvey E. Brazer, *City Expenditures in the United States* (New York: National Bureau of Economic Research, 1959), pp. 61-65, for explanation of his classification of cities. He defines "common functions" to include police and fire protection, highways, recreation, general control, sanitation, health other than hospitals, and general public buildings (p. 3).

5 Brazer's figures are now old, but there is little reason to think that the comparisons made would be substantially different today. For a definition of a Standard Metropolitan Statistical Area, see footnote 4 in Chapter 4.

6 John Pazour, "Local Government Fiscal Conditions," in International City Management Association, *The Municipal Yearbook* (Washington, D.C., 1972), p. 281.

7 Roy W. Bahl, "Studies on Determinants of Public Expenditure: A Review," in Selma J. Mushkin and John Cotton, eds., *Functional Federalism* (Washington, D.C.: George Washington University, 1968), p. 197.

8 For an excellent survey and critical evaluation of various statistical studies, see *ibid.*, pp. 184-203.

9 Edward Banfield, *The Unheavenly City* (Boston: Little Brown, 1970), pp. 36 and 56-64.

10 Welfare districts (which in some cases may be cities like New York City) are required by Federal legislation to meet certain minimum standards, which may be construed as mandated expenses on welfare. In the event they do not meet these standards, they may lose their federal aid.

11 The Conference Board, *Government Services in Major Metropolitan Areas* (New York, 1972).

12 Pazour, *op cit.*, p. 282.

13 William Baumol, "Macroeco-

nomics of Unbalanced Growth: The Anatomy of Urban Crisis," *American Economic Review,* June 1967, pp. 415-26.

14 Note that during this period statistical reporting changed from calendar year to fiscal year.

15 Werner Z. Hirsch, *et al., Fiscal Pressures on the Central City* (New York: Praeger, 1971), p. 5.

16 Note that here we are speaking of spending *in* cities, rather than *by* cities, though for some of the larger cities this distinction is not so important.

17 Phillip E. Vincent, "The Fiscal Impact of Commuters," in Hirsch, *op. cit.,* pp. 41-135.

18 *Ibid.*

19 Henry S. Terrell, "The Fiscal Impact of Nonwhites," in Hirsch, *op. cit.,* pp. 168-69.

20 *Ibid.* pp. 167-78. There seems no reason to presume that present conditions would be substantially different.

21 *Ibid.,* p. 182.

22 *Ibid.,* pp. 197-99.

23 *Ibid.,* pp. 195-97.

24 *Ibid.,* p. 214.

25 Robert F. Adams, "On the Variation in the Consumption of Public Services," in Harvey E. Brazer, ed., *Essays in State and Local Finance* (Ann Arbor, Mich.: Institute of Public Administration, University of Michigan, 1967), p. 18.

26 Using 1960 data for a large number of cities (46) Terrell found

no positive correlation between the percentage of nonwhites in the population and the per capita expenditures for police functions. He did discover, however, that police expenditures did correlate positively and significantly with the rate of recent *increase* in the nonwhite population of our cities. Even this latter argument has been somewhat challenged by Savitz, who studied the crime rates of 900 Negro boys in Philadelphia and found that they were higher among the children of long-time residents than among the newcomers. (Cited in Charles E. Tilley, "Race and Migration to the American City," in James Q. Wilson, ed., *The Metropolitan Enigma,* Washington, D.C., Chamber of Commerce of the United States, 1967.)

27 U.S. Federal Bureau of Investigation, *Uniform Crime Reports for the United States,* 1970, p. 185.

28 Adams, *op. cit.,* p. 22.

29 ACIR, *Fiscal Balance in the American Federal System,* Vol. 2, *Metropolitan Fiscal Disparities* (Washington, D.C. October 1967), p. 31.

30 *Ibid.*

31 U.S. Bureau of the Census, *General Demographic Trends for Metropolitan Areas 1960-1970* (Washington, D.C., 1972).

32 Brazer, *op. cit.,* pp. 54-55.

33 *Ibid.,* pp. 66-67.

3

URBAN

REVENUE

PROBLEMS

Cities are governed by people, and people everywhere have a common problem, that of making ends meet. For nearly all of us our desires exceed our ability to pay. This is true not only of individuals but also of groups. Cities, the aggregates with which we are here concerned, are characteristically made up of people who want to consume collectively more services than current revenues can support. So their officials hunt for the most acceptable ways of getting additional money to spend: finding new taxpayers, adopting the least painful new taxes, raising old tax rates, borrowing, or getting outside aid.

Although this chapter will focus on the advantages and disadvantages of each of these revenue-raising methods, we would do well to keep in mind that the urban fiscal problem is definitely not one-sided. The budgetary crisis is not exclusively a revenue one. Deficits are the result of a subtraction process, expenditures from revenues, and the negative result is due as much to a too large subtrahend (expenditures) as to a too small minuend (revenues). To paraphrase Marshall's famous scissors analogy of the market place: it takes both blades, expenditures and revenues, to do the cutting.

However, in the history of cities as with states and the federal government, the growth in the traditional tax base has rarely proved sufficient to keep up with the desire for more services or the rising cost of providing traditional ones.[1] Therefore rates have to be raised or new sources found.

Tax Alternatives in General

In planning next year's taxes, city fathers first project the revenue yields of existing taxes. For the general property tax, the mainstay of city budgets, that means, chiefly, examining the assessment rolls to see how much new building has taken place. If there is also a sales tax on the books, the national and local trends in consumer spending must be evaluated. Similarly the yield of a personal or business income tax is predicted by considering the secular or even the probable cyclical trend.

If the total of these projections promises to be insufficient to pay for desired and mandated expenditures, then a choice must be made between raising the rate levied against existing tax bases or levying against new ones. The history of urban finance shows that both of these alternatives and more have been adopted by one city or another during their years of fiscal crisis.

Between 1955 and 1972 cities found it necessary to raise 347 percent more revenue, as shown in Table 3.1, and most of this $27 billion increase was raised internally. Some $17.1 billion of the extra money came from taxes and charges imposed by the cities, as compared to only $10 billion from intergovernmental aid. The rate of increase in the latter, however, was 695 percent, versus only a 268 percent increase from "own resources." Similar rates of increase are likely to continue to be necessary. Another inference that can be drawn from the figures in Table 3.1 is that the cities are finding it politically easier to get additional revenues from non-property sources than from the property tax. For instance, the sales and gross receipts tax yields rose 337 percent, while revenues from the property tax rose only 192 percent. Charges and miscellaneous receipts from municipal services (e.g., hospitals, sewerage, air-

TABLE 3.1

Revenues of City Governments, 1955–72
(In millions)

	1955	1972	Percentage Increase, 1955–72
TOTAL GENERAL REVENUES	$7,823	$34,937	347%
A. Total Own Resources	6,385	23,502	268
Taxes	5,100	17,058	234
Property tax	3,767	10,988	192
Sales and gross receipts	728	3,185	337
Licenses and other	606	2,885	376
Current charges and miscellaneous	1,285	6,445	401
B. Intergovernmental Revenues	1,438	11,434	695
From state governments only	1,236	8,377	578
TOTAL DEBT			
Net long-term debt	13,632	42,759	214
Short-term debt	671	6,678	895

SOURCE: U.S. Bureau of the Census, *City Government Finances,* 1955 and 1971–72.

ports) rose 401 percent. The reasons for this change in relative revenue sources will be considered below as each source is discussed.

The General Property Tax

Because of the continuing importance of the general property tax in urban finance, standard texts in urban finance generally examine its advantages and disadvantages in detail. Here our concern is only with the property tax as a potential source of the additional revenues that cities will need in the future to cope with the rising expenditure trend shown in Chapter 2.

We have already noted that cities derived 192 percent more

TABLE 3.2

Increase in Per Capita Revenue in Cities of Various Sizes, 1960–72

Source of Revenue	All Cities	Cities Having Population of:						
		1 Million and Over	500,000–999,999	300,000–499,999	200,000–299,999	100,000–199,999	50,000–99,999	Below 50,000
TOTAL GENERAL REVENUE	163.59%	208.74%	170.68%	177.51%	166.67%	142.94%	118.68%	113.57%
	($264.67)	($620.48)	($387.18)	($295.87)	($285.47)	($251.78)	($201.78)	($138.14)
Own Resources	121.44	127.21	121.63	139.80	110.19	112.43	100.05	102.43
	(178.04)	(363.74)	(245.45)	(203.35)	(188.18)	(177.34)	(151.64)	(106.76)
Taxes	110.87	122.08	103.71	116.04	106.05	110.80	90.25	87.00
	(129.22)	(292.26)	(181.57)	(131.07)	(133.56)	(131.56)	(110.86)	(69.64)
Property tax	85.80	91.45	63.94	84.69	84.19	93.35	74.53	68.10
	(83.24)	(158.14)	(107.28)	(82.26)	(88.98)	(101.12)	(83.74)	(50.06)
Other taxes	179.00	173.71	213.46	202.79	167.27	201.09	163.56	162.47
	(45.98)	(134.12)	(74.29)	(48.81)	(44.94)	(30.44)	(27.12)	(19.58)
Intergovernmental Finances	332.88	528.01	338.93	327.00	455.25	269.25	204.43	159.88
	(86.62)	(256.73)	(141.73)	(92.53)	(97.28)	(74.44)	(50.14)	(31.03)

NOTE: Figures in parenthesis are average per capita revenue for 1971–72.

SOURCE: U.S. Bureau of the Census, City Government Finances, 1960 and 1971–72.

revenue from property taxation in 1972 than in 1955, which is reasonable proof that more money could be obtained from this source in the future. At the same time, there is a clearly discernible trend away from reliance upon it for all increased revenue needs, as shown by its decline from 74 percent of total urban tax revenue in 1955 to 64 percent in 1972. The same trend shows up even more clearly when its yield is compared with total urban revenues from all sources, the drop being from 48 percent to 31 percent. The greater decline in this percentage is due chiefly to the rise in intergovernmental aid to municipalities.

Another overview can be obtained by shifting our approach to a per capita basis and a shorter time period, as in Table 3.2. Data for 1960-72 show an 86 percent rise in city property tax revenues. Other municipal taxes grew more rapidly, 179 percent, and inter-governmental revenues most rapidly of all (333 percent). As a result total per capita revenues for all U.S. cities rose 164 percent. Table 3.2 shows rates of increase for cities of different sizes. Those with a population of a million or more raised their property tax revenues by 91 percent, while the smallest cities, those below 50,000, were showing a rise of only 68 percent per capita.

Cities differ markedly in the extent to which they rely on the property tax to raise desired revenues. Sometimes this is due to differences in the functions assumed at the different levels of government: city, school district, county, and state. In other cases tradition rules, and some older cities like Boston stay with the property tax while younger ones like Los Angeles and Seattle rely more heavily on nonproperty taxes. Whereas in 1971-72, the 48 largest cities used the property tax to provide an average of 43.1 percent of the total raised from their own resources, the figure for Boston was 80.7 percent, for Los Angeles 36.6 percent, and for Seattle 24.8 percent.

Comparisons between cities in the matter of property tax rates in any given year is dangerous because of variations in the ratios of assessed value to full market value. But increases in property tax rates in specific cities from one year to another do furnish a good indication of changes in the extent to which owners of real property

have been required to support city spending. Table 3.3 shows the
wide range of increases in the property tax burden that occurred in
16 major cities in the four-year period 1962-66. (Peculiar budgetary needs may distort the levies in any particular year, as for San
Jose in this table, and suggest an upward trend for a given
interval that is unlikely to be continued.) Analyzing property-tax
rate changes from 1957 to 1965, the ACIR found a median
increase of 25 percent among the central cities of the 36 largest
Standard Metropolitan Statistical Areas.[2]

TABLE 3.3

Increase in Property Tax Rates in Selected Large Cities, 1962–66
*(In descending order of percentage increase; tax rates
per $100 of assessment)*

City	1962	1966	Percentage Increase
San Jose	$1.64	$ 3.20	95.00%
Phoenix	1.60	2.30	43.75
Indianapolis	2.97	3.83	28.96
San Diego	1.53	1.87	22.22
Boston	8.54	10.43	22.13
Los Angeles	1.09	2.04	20.71
Chicago	1.42	1.70	19.72
Oakland	2.75	3.25	18.18
Rochester, N.Y.	4.49	5.30	18.04
Cincinnati	1.24	1.40	12.90
Buffalo	4.40	4.82	9.55
Omaha	1.83	1.98	8.20
Cleveland	1.58	1.68	6.33
Seattle	1.81	1.87	3.31
Milwaukee	2.18	2.25	3.21
Birmingham	1.05	1.07	1.90

NOTE: Property tax rates have been computed by dividing the total property tax revenue by assessed values of property for each city.

SOURCES: Calculated from U.S. Bureau of the Census, *City Government
Finances* for various years; and idem, *Trends in Assessed Valuations and
Sales Ratios, 1956–1966* (Washington, D.C., 1970).

Nonproperty Taxes in Present City Budgets

Considerations of both equity and necessity have led many large cities to make use of nonproperty taxes to meet their revenue needs. Certain expenditures of large cities have already been shown to relate to commuting workers and shoppers. Why not ask them to pay some of the costs by imposing income and sales taxes? The peculiar problems of resort cities also have been mentioned. Surely the convention visitors and recreation seekers who come for short stays can justly be asked to pay special taxes on hotel and motel occupancy plus sales taxes on meals and commodity purchases.

The chief reason for the first city use of taxes on retail sales and personal incomes seems to have been genuine financial need beyond the apparent capacity of property owners to meet. When the City of New York first adopted a retail sales tax in 1934, budgetary pressures were paramount. Philadelphia was in a similar predicament in 1939, when it became the first U.S. city to enact a personal income tax. Real estate tax delinquencies were high and promised to go even higher if property tax rates were raised. The latter threat has often been used to justify the use of nonproperty taxation. "Make someone else share the burden, our taxes are killing us," the real estate owners say.

For these and other reasons almost all large and medium-sized cities in the past 30 years have moved strongly in the direction of nonproperty taxes. A 1968 survey by the International City Management Association showed that out of 270 cities replying, 165 imposed a general retail sales tax, 112 taxed sales of alcoholic beverages, and 46 had a personal income tax; 60 percent of the group raised money from business license taxes of various kinds, usually based on a percentage of gross receipts.[3]

The biggest cities have become the biggest users, as shown by Table 3.4. These figures make abundantly clear that the large cities are the chief users of nonproperty taxes, as they are also the chief spenders. Note that the percentage of total taxes contributed by the general sales tax is slightly higher for cities over 1 million than for smaller cities. In the category of "other taxes and licenses" the contrast between large cities and small becomes still greater. The poor correlation of selective sales tax yields with city size suggests that the introduction of this type of tax was somewhat at random and depended a good deal on local pressures and vested interests.

TABLE 3.4

Nonproperty Taxes As a Percentage of Total Taxes, by Size of Cities, 1972

Cities with 1970 population (in thousands) of:

Tax	All Cities	1,000 & Above	500– 1,000	300– 500	200– 300	100– 200	50– 100	Below 50
General sales	11%	13%	11%	11%	12%	7%	10%	10%
Selective sales	8	8	10	10	9	7	5	7
Other taxes and licenses	17	25	20	16	12	· 9	9	12
Total	36	46	41	37	33	23	24	29

SOURCE: U.S. Bureau of the Census, City Government Finances, 1971–72.

Another way of appreciating the importance of nonproperty taxation is to look at the figures for individual cities, as in Table 3.5. Sixteen large cities, including Detroit, St. Louis, Philadelphia, and Washington, have shifted more than half of their taxation from property to nonproperty bases.

We are also concerned with the trend in yields of the major forms of urban taxation. Recent changes are shown in Table 3.6. The most rapid revenue increase for this period was derived from the personal income tax, followed by selective sales taxes.

The increasing use of nonproperty taxes by the cities has important implications for their overall tax flexibility. The ACIR has estimated income elasticities of major local taxes (i.e., percentage change in tax yield divided by percentage change in income) for different areas for the year 1971. These estimates are given in Table 3.7.

TABLE 3.5

Nonproperty Taxes As a Percentage of Total Tax Collections in 48 Largest Cities, 1970

Under 10%	10–19%	20–29%	30–39%	40–49%	Over 50%
Boston	Buffalo	Baltimore	Chicago	Atlanta	Birmingham
Indianapolis	Minneapolis	Honolulu	Columbus	Cleveland	Cincinnati
Milwaukee	Newark	Memphis	Dallas	Los Angeles	Denver
		Nashville	El Paso	Oakland	Detroit
		Portland	Fort Worth	Pittsburgh	Kansas City
		St. Paul	Houston	San Diego	Long Beach
		San Francisco	Jacksonville	San Jose	Louisville
			Miami		Norfolk
			New Orleans		Oklahoma City
			New York		Philadelphia
			Omaha		Phoenix
			San Antonio		St. Louis
					Seattle
					Toledo
					Tulsa
					Washington, D.C.

SOURCE: Calculated from data in U.S. Bureau of the Census, *City Government Finances, 1969–70.*

TABLE 3.6

City Tax Yields, 1957, 1966–67, and 1971–72
(In millions)

Tax	1957	1966–67	1971–72	Percentage Increase 1957–67	Percentage Increase 1967–72
Property	$4,251	$7,269	$10,988	70.99%	51.16%
Sales and gross receipts	937	1,673	3,185	78.54	90.37
General	601	998	1,866	66.06	86.97
Selective	336	675	1,319	100.89	95.40
Personal income	181	818	—	351.93	—

NOTE: Personal income tax revenue data for 1971–72 are not shown in the source. Other sources of city revenues are omitted from this table; see Table 3.1. Also see Table 5.3, which gives 1971 income tax data for the 48 largest cities.

SOURCE: U.S. Bureau of the Census, *City Government Finances, 1957, 1966–67,* and *1971–72.*

Since the coefficients of income elasticity of nonproperty taxes are greater than those for property tax, the increasing use of nonproperty taxes will increase the overall income elasticity of local taxes and make the tax structure more flexible. This would make revenues from city taxes more responsive to changes in the level of personal income—a very desirable fiscal feature. During inflationary periods, when costs are rising, revenues will also rise without a rate increase.

Revenue benefits from new taxes are not without costs, the most important of which are indirect, at least from the viewpoint of city finance. For instance, what does the first levying of a new tax or the subsequent raising of rates do to the future tax base for that tax or for others upon which the city depends? We have already noted the city dwellers' "flight to the suburbs," for which a high central city property tax is partly responsible. Business firms may also move to suburbs to escape high taxes, both property taxes and nonproperty

TABLE 3.7

Income Elasticities of Major State and Local Taxes
in 1971, Estimated by ACIR

Tax	Area	Income Elasticity
Personal income	Kentucky	1.94
	New York State	1.80
	Hawaii	1.47
General property	New York City	1.41
	Baltimore City	1.25
	Honolulu Co.	0.89
	Multnomah Co., Ore.	0.84
	Jefferson Co., Ky.	0.50
	Newark, N.J.	0.38
	Albany City, N.Y.	0.34
General sales	Maryland	1.08
	Kentucky	0.92

SOURCE: ACIR, *State-Local Finances: Significant Features and Suggested Legislation* (Washington, D.C., 1972). Table 134, p. 301, includes income elasticity estimates in other studies for earlier years and for other governmental units.

taxes. Here again, however, reasons for moving are complex and varied. The most recent tax changes may be merely the last straw, or they may be just the popular whipping boy, while other important forces are not stressed.

In spite of some very obvious, even noisy departures of business firms from central cities and the minor arrival of new ones, fiscal pressures of the moment seem to weigh more heavily on cities than fiscal cautions of the morrow. City after city has levied new taxes, imposed service charges, and raised former tax rates. From the urban fiscal record, none of the nonproperty taxes appears to have been so obnoxious or threatening as to have failed of adoption.

The emigration impulse diminishes as time passes and people get used to the new levies or as nearby suburban communities adopt them too. Aging is not confined to the already old. Nor are the satellite cities immune to an influx of poor people or the depressing effect of factory closings. It's a matter of time and of degree.

THE RETAIL SALES TAX FOR CITIES

In their quest for additional revenue without further burden on the property tax, cities are turning increasingly to the retail sales tax. They are following the example of the states, which much earlier found the property tax inadequate and unsuited to their revenue needs. Because they derive their city charters from the states, cities depend on general or special legislation by the states to permit them to impose new taxes like this one. Only half of the states had done so as of January 1971.

The first city to impose a sales tax was New York in 1934, followed by New Orleans in 1936. After World War II, several states passed permissive legislation, and many of their cities began to exercise their new prerogatives, notably in California and Illinois. The most rapid spread of city sales taxes occurred in the 1960's. At first they were administered locally, but after 1950, following the lead of Mississippi, state administration of local sales taxes became the vogue (19 out of 25 states in 1971). There is good reason for this since it reduces administrative costs where the tax base and the tax-paying units are the same under both state and local systems. John L. Mikesell summarizes: "Most of this growth can be attributed to greater demand for local government services combined with continued dissatisfaction with local property taxes, and the reluctance of legislators to raise state tax rates."[4]

Although American cities are deriving much more revenue from the sales tax, as shown in Table 3.1, some serious students argue that its gradual spread by the separate action of city council after city council is not desirable for several reasons. There is some danger that special interests may succeed in getting rate discriminations in their favor, even total exemptions. In other cases the tax becomes levied on certain producer goods and services and is thus pyramided instead of being confined to retail sales to ultimate consumers. If adjacent cities impose different rates, then shoppers will tend to shift their buying patterns as they do now across state lines when one state has a higher sales tax than another. Some of this is inevitable under fiscal federalism, but, many argue, it is better not compounded. Already mentioned is the greater administrative cost when cities set up their own retail sales taxes instead of operating under a state-wide plan.

A better way to meet the growing revenue needs of cities through the use of the sales tax is to go beyond state administration and collection of local sales taxes to one completely unified system for all municipalities. This would be the state sales tax itself presumably raised at the beginning to the highest prior combined city-state rate and moving up from there. The cities which thus give up that form of taxation would then receive from the state a share of its revenue according to some measure of need. (The revenue-sharing formula might be written to include counties, villages, and unincorporated areas.) Less to be desired in this day of equalizing grants would be the return to each local unit of the exact sum collected within its borders. Overlapping units like counties would have to be excluded from such a plan. The minimum acceptable procedure would be a state law requiring a uniform base for both state and local taxes but permitting autonomy and different rates.[5]

THE PERSONAL INCOME TAX
USED BY CITIES IN DISTRESS

Philadelphia adopted a municipal income tax towards the end of the Great Depression, in 1939, but it was not until after the end of World War II that other important cities took up this method of financing their rising burden. Toledo was the first of 11 medium-sized cities (including St. Louis) to start using a personal income tax between 1946 and 1950. A few more followed suit during the fifties, but the tax didn't really catch on until the sixties, when it was adopted by Detroit, Kansas City, Baltimore, Cleveland, and New York to name some of the biggest. As of the end of 1969, there were 49 cities of 50,000 or more levying an income tax and more than 3,400 smaller cities, school districts, and villages.

The total revenue raised thus far by this form of nonproperty taxation has not been great, only 27 percent of the total tax collections of the 14 largest cities using the tax in 1971-72. But the potential is great, and the personal income tax avoids two of the major defects of the property tax, its regressivity and its adverse effects on the quantity of central city housing. The income tax also avoids a major defect of local sales taxes and other local business taxes. It seems to drive very few people away from central cities when the tax is collected at the source within those cities and thus burdens commuters and local residents alike. Netzer[6] has estimated that if the 43 largest cities in 1965-66 had imposed as little as a 1 percent tax on all personal income earned within the central cities, they would have collected about $1.3 billion, which is more than a third of what their property taxes yielded in that year. Maybe one-fourth of the tax would be paid by commuters, which seems eminently reasonable.

A number of cities presently raise more than Netzer's estimate of one-quarter of total tax revenues from the personal income tax. Four relatively small cities in Ohio raised over 70 percent of their taxes this way: Canton, Columbus, Springfield, and Youngstown. Larger cities raising over 50 percent in 1967-68 included Toledo, Louisville, Flint, and Akron. In 1971-72 Detroit obtained 35 percent, St. Louis 29 percent, and New York City 21 percent. Philadelphia, which started it all, had the highest income tax rate of any large city in the nation, 3 percent, and raised 63 percent of its total tax revenues with this tax.[7]

Even though there are administrative problems with the personal income tax as used by cities and some slight adverse migration effects, they have not deterred cities from adopting it and are not likely to restrain its spread or the imposition of higher rates in the future. Thus far, however, its use is confined largely to the Northeast and North Central parts of the country and as of 1970 was not found on the Pacific Coast.

USER CHARGES AND MISCELLANEOUS FEES
  IN URBAN BUDGETS

A somewhat unappreciated source of urban revenues is the

category of current charges and miscellaneous general revenues. In 1971-72 these amounted to $6.4 billion (or $48.82 per capita) for all cities, which was greater than the total of all nonproperty taxes, $45.98 per capita. More important, perhaps, they amounted to more than half the $83.24 per capita raised from the property tax. A total of this magnitude, even if derived from a congeries of entries, is not to be treated lightly in this day of urban budgetary difficulties.

These charges include the fees and licenses required in the regulatory process. Some are designed to protect consumers, like building permits, registration and inspection of weights and measures, and the like. Others enforce professional standards by excluding unqualified persons from the right to engage in certain occupations. A few are regulatory in the sense that they limit the number who may engage in a line of business, like taxicabs. There are also admission fees to recreational facilities. Charges for sewerage and garbage disposal make users or property owners pay directly for the benefits received. The imposition of user charges should, of course, involve careful consideration of aspects peculiar to each tax method or tax base. These include costs of collection, revenue elasticities, output effects, and, when used as control devices, their net advantages compared with other and more direct approaches.

Intergovernmental Aid to Urban Budgets

Fortunately for city taxpayers, not all the burden of paying for services to city residents falls directly on their backs. Aid from higher levels of government is substantial, both by grants and by the assumption of functions. In 1971-72, for instance, states contributed about 24 percent of the total general revenue of cities and thus bore that much of the load of their expenditures. The big increase in state support came during the Great Depression. Before that time there was some help with school and highway needs, but the total contribution by states was below 10 percent.

Federal aid to cities has also risen markedly, but it is harder to isolate since much of it goes through state governments rather than directly. In 1970 direct federal aid was $1.7 billion, which amounted to 6 percent of city general revenue, up from 2.5 percent in 1955. The states received $20 billion and passed on $6 billion to the cities. The federal government also makes direct disbursements, like Medicaid and Social Security annuities to the aged, that benefit city dwellers in such a way as to reduce the need for spending by city governments.

TABLE 3.8

The Increasing Importance of Intergovernmental Revenues: Per Capita Amounts in City Budgets, 1960–72

Source	1960	1972	Percentage Increase
GENERAL REVENUE	$100.40	$264.67	164%
A. Own Resources	80.39	178.04	121
Taxes	61.28	129.22	111
Property tax	44.80	83.24	86
Sales and gross receipts	10.49	24.13	130
Licenses and others	5.99	21.86	265
Current charges and			
miscellaneous	19.11	48.82	155
B. Intergovernmental Revenue	20.01	86.62	333
Intergovernmental Revenue As Percentage of General Revenue	20%	33%	—

SOURCE: U.S. Bureau of the Census, *City Government Finances,* 1960 and 1971–72.

City budget figures, therefore, show only part of the benefits derived from higher level grants and spending, but amounts received that do pass through the city treasurer's hands clearly ease his problems. These amounts are shown in Table 3.8 for the period 1960-72. Intergovernmental revenues increased more than fourfold on a per capita basis, while total revenues increased less than three-fold. Thus, although local expenditures rose 181 percent during these years, the property tax rose by only 86 percent and other local taxes and charges by 130 percent. Clearly, the local fiscal burden was mitigated substantially by the major increase in aid from above.

TABLE 3.9

Urban Intergovernmental Revenues by City Size

	Per Capita Amount, 1971–72	Percentage Increase, 1960–72
ALL CITIES	$ 86	333%
Over 1 million	256	528
500,000–1 million	141	339
300,000–500,000	92	327
200,000–300,000	97	455
100,000–200,000	74	269
50,000–100,000	50	204
Under 50,000	31	160

SOURCE: Compiled from information in U.S. Bureau of the Census, *City Government Finances,* 1960 and 1971–72.

Intergovernmental revenues were more important for big cities than for small ones in 1971-72. Cities with over a million people received $256 per capita in outside aid, and those with 500,000 to 1 million obtained $141, as compared with a national city average of only $86. This is shown in Table 3.9, where the small amounts reaching citizens in the smaller cities are also detailed (only $31 for the smallest cities and $50 for citizens of cities from 50,000 to 100,000). Similarly, the greatest *rates* of increase were in the largest cities: a whopping 528 percent for the top group,[8] compared with 339 percent in the next, and on down to only a 160 percent gain in the smallest. The very great rise in intergovernmental aid to the top group was undoubtedly the result chiefly of the rise in antipoverty measures during the sixties and the definitely higher percentages of poor people in the major cities. However, we should not overlook the political clout of big cities, both in getting favorable distribution formulae written and in influencing their administration.

Grants-in-aid to cities from higher government levels are chiefly of two types, categorical and general, the latter often called tax sharing or revenue sharing. The former are aimed at specific needs, such as education and highways, and may call for matching funds locally raised. General grants have no strings attached and may be used by the recipient government to pay the expenses of whatever function it wishes, or even to reduce taxes.

Because much federal aid reaches the cities by way of the states, it is of some interest to examine a breakdown of total state-local grants from Washington during the decade of the sixties and to note their different rates of increase. The lines of different steepness in Figure 3.1 indicate the different rates of increase of the indicated categories. (See also Table 3.10.) Commerce and transportation, chiefly highway aid, all of which went to states, was the largest category for most of the period but did not increase rapidly. It was surpassed by income security programs in 1971, chiefly Aid to Families with Dependent Children, most of whom lived in cities. Then in 1972 Congress passed the general revenue-sharing bill, which promised an average of $6 billion a year for five years, with use unrestricted as to category. About a third of that was earmarked for cities. (See Chapter 5 for further discussion.) Back in 1962 direct federal aid to local governments (see Table 3.11) was much less and was used chiefly to stimulate the construction of needed physical facilities.

State aid to municipalities and other local governments now goes chiefly for education, highways, and public welfare, with some for general local government support. Whatever the intent of such aid, it usually is both substitutive and stimulative. That is, state aid to schools usually causes more to be spent on education than otherwise, but not a dollar more for every dollar in aid. Local government may, for instance, increase school spending by only 50 cents for each dollar of aid and use the other fifty cents to reduce school taxes. Or, conceivably, some money might be diverted to a different use. Much depends on the local situation, with presuma-

FIGURE 3.1

Trend of Categorical Federal Aid to State and Local Governments, by Functions, 1961–73
(In millions)

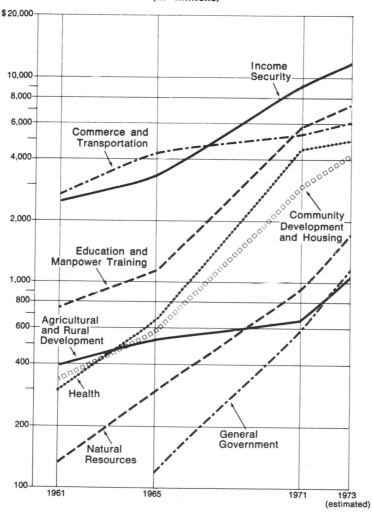

TABLE 3.10

Categorical Federal Aid to State and Local Governments by Major Functions, Selected Fiscal Years, 1961–73

(In millions)

Function	1961	1965	1971	1973 (estimated)	Percentage Increase 1965–73	Percentage Increase 1971–73
Agricultural and rural development	$ 398.2	$ 517.6	$ 659.7	$ 1,060.9	104.9%	60.8%
Natural resources	131.7	298.0	920.4	1,731.7	481.1	88.1
Commerce and transportation	2,668.5	4,397.4	5,299.3	6,016.6	36.8	13.5
Community development and housing	332.1	576.2	2,853.8	4,158.4	621.6	45.7
Education and manpower training	747.5	1,074.9	5,721.9	7,537.8	601.2	31.7
Health	295.6	644.6	4,467.0	4,926.3	664.2	10.2
Income security	2,467.9	3,226.9	9,270.3	11,822.0	266.3	27.5
General government	48.1	122.4	585.5	1,142.7	833.5	95.1
General revenue sharing	—	—	—	7,250.0	—	—
Total *(including minor functions)*	7,112.6	10,903.9	29,844.0	45,728.9	319.3	53.2

SOURCE: Tax Foundation, *Federal Grants: The Need for Reform* (New York, 1973), p. 15.

TABLE 3.11

Direct Federal Aid to Cities, 1962
(In millions)

Construction and operation of schools in federally affected areas	$256
Urban renewal	160
Low rent public housing	149
Construction of waste treatment facilities	42
Construction of airports	33
Miscellaneous	7

SOURCE: ACIR, *The Role of Equalization in Federal Grants* (Washington, D.C., 1964), p. 26.

bly more substitution for taxes resulting in hard-pressed cities and more stimulation of additional local spending in others not feeling so pinched.

There also seem to be different responses in different categories. One study[9] of data for 1960 showed public welfare stimulation to be only 20 cents per dollar of state aid, whereas school spending rose 52 cents, highway 67 cents, and health and hospitals more than $2.50. In the last case, taxes must have been raised as a result of the state aid.

States differ widely in their patterns of per capita aid to local governments, and therefore cities in one state may get a lot more help from above than cities in another. New Hampshire gives very little, for instance, and California gives nine or ten times as much. Some states, like Hawaii, make no grants to localities for education because the school system is almost completely state financed. Nationwide totals and averages hide many important differences.

Notes

1 Although there has been some reduction in the federal personal and corporate income tax rates in recent years for various reasons, including the desire to stimulate the economy, one should note the

steady rise in Social Security tax
rates, whose total revenue doubled
between 1955 and 1971.

2 ACIR, *Fiscal Balance in the American Federal System,* Vol. 2,
Metropolitan Fiscal Disparities
(Washington, D.C., 1967), p.
91.

3 John Pazour, "Local Government
Fiscal Conditions," in International City Management Association, *The Municipal Yearbook*
(Washington, D.C., 1972), p.
283.

4 Mikesell, "Local Government
Sales Taxes," in John F. Due, ed.,
State and Local Sales Taxes,
(Chicago: Public Administration
Service, 1971), p. 267.

5 *Ibid.,* p. 322.

6 U.S. Congress, Joint Economic
Committee, *Impact of the Property
Tax: Its Economic Implications for*

Urban Problems, 1968, p. 40.

7 ACIR, *The Commuter and the
Municipal Income Tax* (Washington, D.C., 1970), pp. 9-11; and
U.S. Bureau of the Census, *City
Government Finances,* 1971-1972
(Washington, D.C., 1973), pp.
87-98.

8 Because of its large size, New York
City's figures dominate the category of cities over a million, but its
per capita rate of increase of intergovernmental aid during the sixties (559%) was less than that of
Philadelphia (728%).

9 Seymour Sacks and Robert Harris,
"The Determinants of State and
Local Government Expenditures
and Intergovernmental Flow of
Funds," *National Tax Journal,*
Vol. 17, No. 1, March 1964, p.
83.

4

CITIES

AND

THEIR

SUBURBS

Growth and Decay

All living things have a cycle of life. They are born, develop, grow
to maturity, decline, and die. Life spans differ in length, from the
short-lived bacteria to the long-lived bristle-cone pines. During
their lives organisms usually give life to successors whose life span
may overlap theirs. Groups of living things have somewhat similar
life cycles, often very much longer than the individual beings of
which they are comprised. Forests, families, dynasties, nations,
species—and cities.

Cities beget suburbs, which grow into small cities, which then
show the vigor of youth, the stability of middle age, and eventual
decline. Jersey City and Hoboken outside of New York City are
good examples. Some cities have longer periods of growth and
prosperity than others, discovering sources of vitality in diversity,
like the cities Jane Jacobs describes with approval.[1] Others
specialize and show superior strength for a while but then, with the
decline in their specialty, age quickly (Seattle, with its overwhelm-
ing dependence on the aircraft industry, is an example). Rather
than dying and disappearing, however, they seem to wither on the
vine.

The fiscal crises of cities are not always associated with age, or with size, but it is safe to say that most of the cities of our nation that appear to be in financial distress are either relatively large or relatively old. Larger cities seem to attract the poor and retain the aged, especially unrelated elderly individuals. Older cities have older buildings, themselves toward the end of their cycles of useful life. Maintenance costs increase for aging people and aging structures. So too for the vital water mains, sewers, and streets of the metropolis. While older people and cities don't have the capital-accumulation problems of the younger, they have greater costs of repair and replacement. And they often call on their more vigorous progeny and associates for financial help.

That is why it seems appropriate to include in a book on the fiscal problems of cities a chapter on the various relations between cities and their suburbs—genetic, symbiotic, parasitic, placental, or commensal. The parent-child analogy seems most appropriate for both biological (population origin) and economic (dependence) reasons. Our older cities are now declining and becoming less able to care for themselves. Their waning vigor is shown in many ways. Nearly all the major cities over 100,000 in the oldest part of the country, the Northeast, have been declining in population since 1950, and some since 1940. The same is true of almost as high a percentage of midwestern cities when we omit those that grew through annexation. The list includes such important cities as Chicago, St. Louis, Detroit, and Cleveland. In the later-blooming South and the younger West, population declines are much less frequent.

Another evidence of waning vigor throughout the older cities is the decline in the percentage of white population during the sixties, down 19 percent in northeastern cities, and the rising percentage of nonwhites, up 25 percent. Most of the latter were immigrants from the rural South whose per capita productivity and tax-paying ability was less than that of the whites whom they displaced. From 1959 to 1968 median family incomes rose only 16 percent in central cities compared to 25 percent in suburbs. Older central cities also have older inhabitants. In 1970, 11 percent of the population of central cities was 65 or older. In their younger suburbs the figure was only 8 percent senior citizens. Old people put a strain on city budgets, bringing more expense and less tax-paying ability. The 1970 Census Employment Survey shows that 55 percent of the elderly unrelated individuals in our inner cities were poor, which is more than the national average.[2]

Average household income in 1970, according to *Sales Management's* 1971 annual survey of buying power, was $10,325 in 19 big cities of the Northeast as opposed to $13,098 in their surrounding suburbs. In the younger areas of the country the "central city" (hereafter referred to as CC) versus "outside central city" (hereafter referred to as OCC) income spread was not so great, only 7 percent in 14 western cities instead of the 26 percent differential in the Northeast. Another way of seeing the CC/OCC income differences is to look at the percentage of households with incomes under $3,000 and over $10,000. For the older Northeast the figures in 1970 were CC 16 percent and OCC 9 percent under $3,000, a clear indication of relative CC poverty. Above $10,000, the percentages were reversed, 33 percent and 46 percent, respectively, showing relative OCC affluence. The same pattern, though less extreme, was repeated in the other regions of the country.

The life cycle of cities was studied for an earlier period (essentially 1948-63) by David L. Birch in his 1970 paper for the Committee for Economic Development.[3] By selecting a sample of 73 Standard Metropolitan Statistical Areas (hereafter referred to as SMSA)[4] to include those of different sizes and ages (based on when first classified as SMSA's), he was able to demonstrate some significant relationships. Between 1948 and 1963 the older cities lost jobs in the fields of retail trade and manufacturing as these activities moved to residential and cheap land areas in the suburbs. The smaller old cities were hurt more than the large ones. Substantial growth occurred in urban service employment and some in wholesaling, but much less rapidly in the older than in the younger SMSA's. Young SMSA central cities resemble the suburbs of the older cities in that they still have some undeveloped land and also relatively ample streets and highways to move cars and trucks to shopping centers and factories. As noted earlier, the shift of economic activity from cities to suburbs reduces the revenue base of central cities without a corresponding reduction in demand for government services. Though the change, fortunately, is more gradual, it resembles the budget crisis in a family when one working member retires or loses his job while the general need for food, shelter, and clothing continues as before.

One of Birch's findings that deserves attention is that the black population of suburbs has recently grown at a more rapid rate than that of central cities, where in some cases it has actually declined.[5] As the suburban fringes of our older cities themselves decay, whites move farther out, and some of the least poor in urban ghettos emigrate to replace them. Upper and middle class blacks are also more numerous than they used to be. It is much the same pattern as that which Banfield describes as the typical history of any city during its spread outward from the original center.[6]

Another Birch argument seems less soundly based. He presents figures showing that between 1959 and 1967 there was a decrease in the percentage of central city families in the poverty and near poverty groups,[7] implying that this has reduced fiscal pressures, which of course it hasn't. General aspirations for the poor and their own demands for better support have risen more rapidly than their incomes, widening the fiscal gap, not narrowing it. This is one illustration of the "revolution of rising expectations." At the other end of the income scale Birch sees a big rise in the percentage of families with incomes over $10,000 and ascribes this to a return of the affluent to the central city to take advantage of its demands for specialists in certain managerial and professional services together with improved living conditions as slums are replaced by modern apartments. A more likely explanation for the statistical shift he observed is the general upward trend in incomes and prices. For instance, between 1960 and 1970 for the country as a whole (not just his sample of 73 SMSA's), families with incomes above $10,000 rose from 14 percent to 49 percent. If central cities

participated less than proportionately in this trend toward affluence, they would appear absolutely better off while declining
relative to their suburbs and the rest of the country.

Special Classes of Suburbs

Obviously, there are different classes of suburb. We have already commented about some of the differences between those in
the older Northeast and those in the West. A general distinction
can also be made between industrial suburbs and residential, or
"bedroom," suburbs. One approach to this classification is
through the figures on assessed value of the different types of
property. The data in Table 4.1 suggest how great the variation is
across the country.

TABLE 4.1

**Suburban Industrial-Commercial Property As a Percentage
of Total Suburban Property, Assessed Value in 1962**
(Suburbs of 22 large SMSA's in descending order of industrialization)

Suburbs of:	Industrial-Commercial Property	Suburbs of:	Industrial-Commercial Property
Pittsburgh	31.2%	San Francisco-Oakland	17.2%
Denver	27.2	New York	17.0
Buffalo	24.9	Louisville	16.4
Rochester	21.8	Chicago	16.3
Kansas City	20.4	Baltimore	16.3
Los Angeles-Long Beach	19.9	San Diego	14.4
Cleveland	19.8	Seattle-Everett	14.2
St. Louis	18.6	Washington, D.C.	12.0
Philadelphia	18.1	Indianapolis	10.9
Cincinnati	17.9	New Orleans	9.8
Newark	17.9	San Antonio	9.0

SOURCE: ACIR, *Fiscal Balance in the American Federal System*, Vol. 2,
Metropolitan Fiscal Disparities (Washington, D.C., 1967), p. 110.

TABLE 4.2

Per Capita Total Expenditures in Central Cities and Outside Central Cities, 1970
(37 largest SMSA's in descending order of ratio, CC/OCC)

SMSA	Per Capita Expenditure CC	OCC	Ratio: CC/OCC
Cincinnati	$ 761	$262	291
Washington, D.C.	1,006	425	237
Baltimore	638	349	183
Atlanta	554	315	176
Newark	735	441	167
Denver	502	306	164
St. Louis	463	292	158
Philadelphia	495	325	152
Portland	486	328	148
Providence-Pawtucket-Warwick	392	265	148
Pittsburgh	450	309	146
Boston	531	365	146
Kansas City	485	347	140
Cleveland	512	368	139
New York	894	644	139
Chicago	478	346	138
Columbus (Ohio)	398	290	137
San Francisco-Oakland	768	596	129
Tampa-St. Petersburg	372	288	129
Rochester	699	549	127
Dallas	352	279	126
Miami	481	387	124
San Bernardino-Riverside-Ontario	635	522	122
Los Angeles-Long Beach	624	529	118
Indianapolis	355	306	116
Milwaukee	562	486	116
Seattle-Everett	524	471	111
Anaheim-Santa Ana-Garden Grove	410	373	110
Minneapolis-St. Paul	540	520	104
New Orleans	334	325	103
Detroit	474	462	103
San Diego	484	472	103
Buffalo	528	520	102
Houston	305	307	99
Phoenix	375	387	97
Paterson-Clifton-Passaic	381	418	91
San Jose	553	612	90

SOURCE: Calculated from data in Seymour Sacks and John Callahan, "Central City Suburban Fiscal Disparity," in ACIR, *City Financial Emergencies: The Intergovernmental Dimension* (Washington, D.C., 1973), Tables B-14 and B-21, pp. 123, 131, 133.

The suburbs of Pittsburgh and Denver are obviously not in the same class with those of New Orleans and San Antonio, the former being highly industrialized and the latter chiefly residential. Sometimes the differences result from the arbitrary county-line boundaries chosen by the Bureau of the Census in defining its Standard Metropolitan Statistical Areas. In other cases cities have expanded by annexation to include much residential land within their own borders. In spite of these statistical problems, aggregation enables us to draw some useful conclusions about the sources of the fiscal difficulties of most of the cities in the United States in the sixties and seventies.

Differences in the Costs of Government in Central Cities and Suburbs

The per capita expenditures of governments are almost everywhere higher in central cities than in their suburbs. Census Bureau data for 1970 show that for the 72 largest SMSA's the weighted average ratio of CC to OCC expenditures was 139/100 per capita. A "ratio" over 100 was registered for 63 out of the 72.[8] The highest was 291/100 (Cincinnati SMSA); the lowest was only slightly below 100 (the SMSA of Allentown-Bethlehem-Easton in Pennsylvania at just below 90). Among the others with more spending per capita outside the central city than within, Houston (1970, pop. 1,233,000) is the only really large city. Table 4.2 presents a short list to reveal the wide range in the CC/OCC ratio from high to low.

This table is useful also in revealing the wide range in per capita expenditures themselves. For central cities the range is from Washington, D.C., with $1,006 in 1970 to Houston with only $305. As is to be expected, most of the low spending cities are in the South; they average about 70 percent of the per capita expenditures of the northeastern cities.

TABLE 4.3

Per Capita Noneducational Expenditures in Central Cities
and Outside Central Cities, 1970
(37 largest SMSA's in descending order of ratio, CC/OCC)

SMSA	Per Capita Expenditure CC	OCC	Ratio: CC/OCC
Washington, D.C.	$745	$181	412
Cincinnati	418	131	319
Baltimore	416	134	310
Denver	332	111	299
St. Louis	287	105	273
Atlanta	336	124	271
Philadelphia	321	122	263
Portland	298	115	259
Columbus	265	111	239
Pittsburgh	296	129	230
Newark	519	236	220
New York	679	312	218
Providence-Pawtucket-Warwick	253	119	213
Rochester	474	224	212
Boston	392	188	209
Kansas City	316	153	207
Chicago	320	147	206
Anaheim-Santa Ana-Garden Grove	221	114	194
Seattle-Everett	374	196	191
Indianapolis	211	112	188
Milwaukee	379	236	184
Cleveland	302	173	172
Dallas	210	123	171
San Francisco-Oakland	559	332	168
Minneapolis-St. Paul	386	236	164
Miami	279	185	151
Detroit	297	201	148
Tampa-St. Petersburg	210	128	144
Los Angeles-Long Beach	431	303	142
Buffalo	363	259	140
Houston	165	122	135
San Bernardino-Riverside-Ontario	368	290	127
San Diego	298	245	122
Phoenix	176	160	110
Paterson-Clifton-Passaic	240	221	109
San Jose	321	307	105
New Orleans	208	202	105

SOURCE: Calculated from data in Seymour Sacks and John Callahan, "Central City Suburban Fiscal Disparity," in ACIR, *City Financial Emergencies: The Intergovernmental Dimension* (Washington, D.C., 1973), Tables B-15 and B-21, pp. 124, 131, 133.

EXPLAINING DIFFERENCES IN SPENDING

The chief reason that central cities spend more per capita on government than do surrounding areas is the desire for more police and fire protection services. This can be seen by dividing all government spending into two parts: education and noneducation. Noneducational expenditures in 1970 were approximately twice as high in our big cities as in their suburbs. Education cost about 15 percent less, not enough of a favorable difference to overcome the much greater amounts spent on noneducational functions. Table 4.3 ranks 37 major SMSA's in order of their CC/OCC ratios for noneducational expenditures in 1970.

As one would expect, the highest expenditure figures in this table are for New York and for Washington, D.C., both with extraordinary policing problems. They have extensive slums and near slums where fire hazards and welfare costs are high as also in certain other cities like Newark. The lowest figures for this group are those for Houston, Phoenix, and southern cities generally, with their smaller size, lower pay scales, and weaker demand functions. Other components of the noneducation group include hospitals and housing, both of which are of distinctly less importance in the smaller cities. Per capita spending on highways and parks and recreation is about the same in dollar amounts, though higher in percentages. Table 4.4 shows the per capita amounts and the relative percentages in the over 1 million group as compared with the 50,000-100,000 group of cities, a size more characteristic of the suburbs.

The cities with the biggest noneducational expenditures per capita also are near the top of the ratio list (Table 4.3). All those over $400 except San Francisco and Los Angeles come in the top 16. The large California cities are the only ones that seem out of place, with high central city spending and low differentials compared with their suburbs. This probably reflects a greater similarity in the income levels of CC and OCC than elsewhere. That Washington, D.C., is at the top of the ratio list is no surprise, since it is surrounded by a ring of wealthy, low density, suburbs. The richest counties in the United States—Montgomery,

TABLE 4.4

Per Capita Total Spending of Big Cities Compared with Small, 1971–72

	Big Cities		Small Cities	
	Per Capita Amount	Percentage of Total Budget	Per Capita Amount	Percentage of Total Budget
Education	$125.14	19.66%	$37.29	17.71%
Welfare	120.43	18.92	2.95	1.40
Police	64.57	10.15	23.54	11.18
Fire	27.00	4.24	18.63	8.85
Highways	19.10	3.00	21.66	10.29
Hospitals	56.48	8.88	6.81	3.23
Parks	13.21	2.08	13.28	6.31
Interest on debt	24.73	3.89	8.41	3.99
Sanitation	19.47	3.06	8.65	4.11
Health	19.60	3.08	2.02	0.96
Housing and urban renewal	31.81	5.00	8.65	4.11

SOURCE: U.S. Bureau of the Census, *City Government Finances*, 1971–72. See our Chapter 2 for explanation of exclusions and intergovernmental aid components.

Maryland, and Fairfax, Virginia—are among them. Moreover Washington, D.C., differs from other cities in having to include in its budget various expenditures that for other cities are partly or wholly assumed by the counties or states of which they are a part. Welfare, highways, and some health expenditures are illustrations.

When we turn to educational expenditures (see Table 4.5), the balance is reversed. Suburbs spend more per capita on public schools than do central cities. Furthermore, the range of the CC/OCC ratios is narrower, only two to one as compared to three to one for noneducational spending ratios (or four to one if Washington, D.C., is included).

A very important difference between CC's and OCC's in regard

TABLE 4.5

Per Capita Educational Expenditures in Central Cities
and Outside Central Cities, 1970
(37 largest SMSA's in descending order of ratio, CC/OCC)

Per Capita Expenditure

SMSA	CC	OCC	Ratio: CC/OCC
San Bernardino-Riverside-Ontario	$267	$232	115
Atlanta	218	191	114
Cleveland	210	195	108
Washington, D.C.	261	244	107
Newark	216	205	105
Cincinnati	137	131	104
New Orleans	126	123	102
Baltimore	215	215	100
Tampa-St. Petersburg	162	162	100
Miami	202	202	100
Providence-Pawtucket-Warwick	139	146	95
St. Louis	176	187	94
Dallas	142	156	91
Portland	188	213	88
Denver	170	195	87
Kansas City	169	194	87
Phoenix	199	227	87
Philadelphia	174	203	86
Pittsburgh	154	180	85
Los Angeles-Long Beach	193	227	85
San Diego	186	227	82

(continued on next page)

to public spending on education arises from the degrees of use of private schools. In big cities, there tends to be a high percentage of nonwhite children from disadvantaged backgrounds. In the eyes of many middle and upper class whites this creates an undesirable school environment for their own children, who, as a result, are sent to private, often segregated, schools. Cities also tend to have more parochial schools than suburbs. Here we have a major reason for smaller per capita spending on public schools in cities than in

TABLE 4.5 (continued)

Per Capita Expenditure

SMSA	CC	OCC	Ratio: CC/OCC
Chicago	158	199	79
San Francisco-Oakland	209	264	79
Boston	139	177	78
Houston	140	185	76
San Jose	232	305	76
Indianapolis	144	194	74
Columbus (Ohio)	133	179	74
Anaheim-Santa Ana-Garden Grove	189	259	73
Milwaukee	183	250	73
Paterson-Clifton-Passaic	141	197	71
Rochester	225	325	69
Detroit	177	261	68
Buffalo	165	261	63
Minneapolis-St. Paul	154	284	54
Seattle-Everett	150	275	54
New York	173	332	52

NOTE: To improve comparability among cities, we have deducted higher education expenditure from the budgets of Baltimore, Cincinnati, and New York, the only ones in which this item appeared.

SOURCE: Calculated from data in Seymour Sacks and John Callahan, "Central City Suburban Fiscal Disparity," in ACIR, *City Financial Emergencies: The Intergovernmental Dimension* (Washington, D.C., 1973), Tables B-16 and B-21, pp. 126, 131, 133.

surrounding areas. By calculating *per pupil* expenditures and comparing, we get corroborative evidence. The CC/OCC ratios are higher and show 15 cities over 100 instead of only 7. Table 4.6 shows the comparative ratios. San Bernardino is the only case in which a shift from per capita to per pupil educational expenditures does not cause an increase in the ratio of city to suburban educational spending.

Education costs tend to be high in large cities partly because of the more expensive vocational schooling required for the high

TABLE 4.6

Educational Expenditure Ratios Per Capita and Per Pupil, 1970
(For the 15 SMSA's with a per pupil ratio above 100)

SMSA	CC/OCC Expenditure Ratio	
	Per Pupil	Per Capita
Cincinnati	305	262
Washington, D.C.	132	107
Atlanta	131	114
Miami	127	100
Cleveland	118	108
Denver	115	87
New Orleans	115	102
San Francisco-Oakland	115	79
San Bernardino-Riverside-Ontario	112	115
St. Louis	111	94
Baltimore	110	103
Providence-Pawtucket-Warwick	110	95
Tampa-St. Petersburg	102	100
Los Angeles-Long Beach	102	85
Philadelphia	101	86

NOTE: The per capita ratios for Cincinnati and Baltimore will be reduced to 104 and 100 respectively if expenditure on higher education is deducted from the budget of these cities.

SOURCE: Calculated from data in Seymour Sacks and John Callahan, "Central City Suburban Fiscal Disparity," in ACIR, City Financial Emergencies: The Intergovernmental Dimension (Washington, D.C., 1973), Table B-16, p. 126.

percentages of poor people, especially nonwhites, and partly because of generally high salary scales in schools. They are high in affluent suburbs because of parental desire for more than the four "R's." Of course, these are low level generalizations with many local exceptions. Fiscal disparities may exist because of such things as attitude differences of taxpayers toward educating other people's children, the more wealthy sometimes seeing themselves being forced to pay for a function which, unlike fire and police protection, seems of little benefit to themselves. Racial and religious feelings may also be present with greater intensity in one city or suburb than another.

Tax Burden Differences

If local governments paid the entire bill for the services they render their citizens, fiscal disparities on the revenue side would be quite similar to those on the expenditure side, but they do not. States finance a major share of educational costs, and the federal government pays a substantial part of the outlays for that group of functions popularly combined under the "welfare" heading. Differences in state policies toward helping local governments are one reason why intercity comparisons of tax burdens on a national basis are not very fruitful. Within a given state, however, comparisons may be more valid, especially if there are several CC/OCC situations that can be compared. In that case ratio differences in per capita local taxes may arise from varying "need" levels and degrees of affluence. In central cities high per capita property values tend to be offset by high percentages of poor people, slum housing, aging municipal facilities, congested streets, and so on. In some suburbs, however, the fortunate accident of having a major utility property or factory may permit lower tax rates for homeowners there than in predominantly bedroom communities with the same level of municipal services.

The fiscal disparities in intergovernmental aid to cities as compared to their suburbs is very pronounced, as shown in Table 4.7. Fifteen cities, including large ones like Los Angeles and Houston, received less per capita from federal and state governments than did their suburbs. Only two of them were in the older Northeast, Buffalo and Rochester. At the top in terms of more favored positions than their suburbs were the Northeastern cities of Boston, Washington, Newark, Baltimore, and Paterson. Also in the more-than-twice-as-much category was Cincinnati, and just below

TABLE 4.7

Per Capita Federal-State Aid to Cities and Suburbs, 1970
(37 largest SMSA's in ascending order of ratio, CC/OCC)

SMSA	CC/OCC Aid Ratio	Population CC (in thousands)	SMSA	CC/OCC Aid Ratio	Population CC (in thousands)
Phoenix	58	582	Pittsburgh	117	520
Dallas	77	844	St. Louis	119	622
Minneapolis-St. Paul	78	744	Portland	123	383
Houston	84	1,233	San Bernardino-Riverside-Ontario	129	308
Seattle-Everett	85	584	Cleveland	132	751
New Orleans	86	593	Detroit	144	1,511
Milwaukee	89	717	San Francisco-Oakland	148	1,077
Kansas City	90	507	Philadelphia	152	1,949
Indianapolis	91	745	Providence-Pawtucket-Warwick	156	340
Los Angeles-Long Beach	92	3,175	Denver	159	515
Buffalo	92	463	Chicago	170	3,367
Anaheim-Santa Ana-Garden Grove	94	446	New York	178	7,895
San Diego	96	697	Cincinnati	222	453
Columbus (Ohio)	97	540	Paterson-Clifton-Passaic	234	282
Rochester	99	296	Baltimore	259	906
San Jose	101	446	Newark	271	382
Atlanta	102	497	Washington, D.C.	303	757
Miami	106	335	Boston	307	641
Tampa-St. Petersburg	110	494			

SOURCES: Calculated from data in Seymour Sacks and John Callahan, "Central City Suburban Fiscal Disparity," in ACIR, *City Financial Emergencies: The Intergovernmental Dimension* (Washington, D.C., 1973), Table B-24, pp. 139–40; and U.S. Bureau of the Census, *Statistical Abstract of the United States, 1972*, pp. 21–23.

that level, New York and Chicago. Assuming that intergovernmental aid is in proportion to need as perceived by Congress and by the state legislatures that write the distribution formulas, these older central cities seem to be less well off than their suburbs and in need of more assistance.

Differences in intergovernmental aid per capita also account for some of the tax burden differences. In Baltimore such aid amounted to more than half of the total expenditure by the city in 1970. Table 4.8 shows that there were 6 other cities in the top 37 SMSA's getting 40 percent or more, while 5 got less than 20 percent. Cities in states with generous state aid programs rank high in Table 4.8: note that the 6 California and 3 New York cities all fall in the 34-45 percent range. In contrast, aid to the 3 large cities in Ohio was much lower, between 17 and 23 percent of their total expenditures. The per capita dollar amount of intergovernmental aid is roughly in the same descending order as aid percentages of city budgets with only a few notable exceptions like Washington, D.C., and Rochester on the high side and Phoenix on the low side. Washington, D.C., of course, is different, being a city-state. Rochester, in New York with its high state aid programs, contrasts with Phoenix in Arizona.

If we now divide intergovernmental aid into its two parts, some interesting differences can be discerned between the way states deal with the CC/OCC problem and the way the federal government handles it. Since state aid is predominantly for education and is designed to give the weaker districts the most help, the choice of measures of fiscal capacity are all important. Where assessed valuation of real property is the chief criterion, OCC's are likely to get more aid per capita than central cities, since the latter have higher land values and more buildings, even if their structures are older. If the measure is per capita income, the neediest portion of SMSA's will be the CC's in the Northeast and in most of the Midwest, but OCC's in the West and most of the South. Shifting the base to income per household instead of per capita would benefit most of the central cities in every region of the country, even the South, since central cities contain more single-person

TABLE 4.8

State-Federal Aid As a Percentage of Total Expenditure of Central Cities, 1970
(37 largest SMSA's in descending order of percentages)

SMSA	Per Capita Aid	Percentage of Total Expenditure
Baltimore	$329	52%
San Bernardino-Riverside-Ontario	278	44
New York	385	43
Boston	224	42
Phoenix	121	42
Detroit	189	40
San Diego	194	40
Buffalo	207	39
San Francisco-Oakland	298	39
Anaheim-Santa Ana-Garden Grove	157	38
Newark	276	38
San Jose	207	37
Washington, D.C.	358	36
Milwaukee	199	35
Los Angeles-Long Beach	209	34
Paterson-Clifton-Passaic	131	34
Rochester	235	34
Minneapolis-St. Paul	177	33
Tampa-St. Petersburg	119	32
Chicago	146	31
Denver	149	30
New Orleans	100	30
Providence-Pawtucket-Warwick	111	29
Miami	137	28
Philadelphia	134	27
Portland	125	26
Seattle-Everett	137	26
Pittsburgh	111	25
Indianapolis	85	24
Cincinnati	171	23
St. Louis	99	22
Houston	61	20
Columbus (Ohio)	75	19
Kansas City	90	19
Atlanta	97	18
Cleveland	87	17
Dallas	54	15

SOURCE: Calculated from data in Seymour Sacks and John Callahan, "Central City Suburban Fiscal Disparity," in ACIR, *City Financial Emergencies: The Intergovernmental Dimension* (Washington, D.C., 1973), Tables B-20 and B-23, pp. 130–31, 137–38.

TABLE 4.9

Per Capita Educational Aid by States to Central Cities and Outside Central Cities, 1970
(37 largest SMSA's in descending order of ratio, CC/OCC)

SMSA	Per Capita Aid CC	OCC	Ratio: CC/OCC
Newark	$ 84	$ 39	215
Philadelphia	95	64	148
Paterson-Clifton-Passaic	42	34	124
Chicago	63	56	113
Cleveland	36	33	109
Detroit	95	89	107
San Diego	88	86	102
Tampa-St. Petersburg	101	101	100
Miami	120	120	100
San Bernardino-Riverside-Ontario	111	113	97
Baltimore	75	81	93
Portland	61	69	88
Atlanta	69	79	87
Pittsburgh	64	76	84
San Jose	96	114	84
Providence-Pawtucket-Warwick	37	45	82
Houston	56	70	80
New Orleans	59	75	79
San Francisco-Oakland	69	91	76
Indianapolis	52	69	75
New York	101	137	74
Anaheim-Santa Ana-Garden Grove	79	108	73
Denver	49	67	73
Dallas	46	65	71
St. Louis	52	73	71
Los Angeles-Long Beach	62	89	70
Milwaukee	40	57	70
Buffalo	94	138	68
Kansas City	51	80	64
Boston	24	39	62
Rochester	98	162	60
Washington, D.C.	49	83	59
Phoenix	79	140	56
Columbus (Ohio)	25	47	53
Cincinnati	36	70	51
Minneapolis-St. Paul	51	118	43
Seattle-Everett	60	141	43

SOURCE: Calculated from data in Seymour Sacks and John Callahan, "Central City Suburban Fiscal Disparity," in ACIR, *City Financial Emergencies: The Intergovernmental Dimension* (Washington, D.C.: 1973), Table B-25, pp. 141–42.

households than do suburbs. Figures on the amount of state educational aid per capita for CC's and OCC's are given in Table 4.9. Except in a few of the older northern cities, the suburban areas are clearly favored because of the greater weight given to assessed value per capita in state aid formulas.

For federal aid the picture is clear. Most of it goes for "welfare," and therefore the higher percentage of poor people and families in central cities makes these the major destination. The 1972 bill for general revenue sharing uses a formula based both on capacity as measured by per capita income and on revenue effort. The former criterion was intended to favor the poorer cities and, to a lesser degree, poor rural areas. The latter resembles the aid-matching requirements of many categorical grants. The net effect of these recent changes in aid programs on CC/OCC ratios is not yet clear. See Chapter 5 for further discussion on the new revenue-sharing programs.

RELATIVE TAX BURDENS

The mixture of federal and state aid is not so important as the total amount per capita of the tax burden that remains. This is the crucial element in the fiscal distress of our cities. How much must the central cities raise in relation to the demands upon the taxpayers in their suburbs? The figures clearly show the relative disadvantage of central cities. For 72 SMSA's in 1970 the unweighted average tax burden was $235 per capita in CC's and $181 in OCC's, or 129:100. The details for the 37 largest are given in Table 4.10. In all except 5 of these the tax burden per capita was clearly heavier in central cities than in suburbs.

There seems to be no positive correlation between size and absolute tax burden per capita. The 3 most populous cities in the country, New York, Chicago, and Los Angeles, were well down the list, while Philadelphia and San Francisco-Oakland were near the middle and Washington, D.C., distinctly different from the others, at the top. Seven out of the first 11 with most adverse tax positions as compared to their environs were in the South or near-South.

TABLE 4.10

Per Capita Taxes Collected by Central Cities and Outside
Central Cities, 1970
(37 largest SMSA's in descending order of ratio, CC/OCC)

SMSA	Taxes Per Capita CC	Taxes Per Capita OCC	Relative Tax Burden, CC/OCC
Washington, D.C.	$516	$231	223
Atlanta	252	122	207
Dallas	211	107	197
Cincinnati	251	134	187
Pittsburgh	294	161	183
Tampa-St. Petersburg	170	95	179
Milwaukee	306	179	171
Portland	260	153	170
Kansas City	253	157	161
New Orleans	148	93	159
St. Louis	267	174	153
Denver	272	180	151
Indianapolis	226	151	150
Minneapolis-St. Paul	227	152	149
San Francisco-Oakland	436	305	143
Boston	369	263	140
Philadelphia	250	180	139
Miami	221	160	138
Cleveland	296	230	129
Seattle-Everett	203	163	125
Columbus (Ohio)	198	162	122
Detroit	255	210	121
Los Angeles-Long Beach	329	272	121
Newark	352	294	120
Providence-Pawtucket-Warwick	196	165	119
Phoenix	172	151	114
Rochester	272	240	113
Baltimore	221	195	113
New York	384	356	108
Houston	181	172	105
San Diego	206	198	104
San Bernardino-Riverside-Ontario	261	257	102
Buffalo	236	238	99
Chicago	244	251	97
Anaheim-Santa Ana-Garden Grove	235	249	94
San Jose	250	295	84
Paterson-Clifton-Passaic	221	278	79

SOURCE: Calculated from data in Seymour Sacks and John Callahan,
"Central City Suburban Fiscal Disparity," in ACIR, *City Financial Emer-
gencies: The Intergovernmental Dimension* (Washington, D.C., 1973),
Table B-18, p. 128.

One must be careful not to assume that high aid ratios usually mean low tax burden ratios. Quite the contrary. It is when there are high tax burdens that aid is most needed. Table 4.11 shows how frequently the same cities, worse off than their suburbs in terms of expenditure ratios, are also worse off by tax burden ratios even though they are better off in terms of aid ratios. Notable exceptions are Atlanta, Kansas City, Columbus, Detroit, and Dallas for intergovernmental aid and Baltimore, Newark, Providence, New Orleans, and Chicago for tax burdens.

Populous Hinterlands As a Cause of Expenditure

In Chapter 2 we described the argument of Brazer and others that the amount of noneducational spending by a city is a direct function of the ratio of population in surrounding areas to that of the central city itself. Kee's analysis of 1962 data showed that the more commuters who come and go from the suburbs the more fiscal effort has to be made by central cities.[9]

A Summary of Fiscal Disparities Between Cities and Suburbs

The foregoing analysis of urban fiscal problems in comparison with those of their suburbs has been based largely on data contained in a report prepared for the ACIR in 1973 by Seymour Sacks and John Callahan.[10] We have used it to make our points because its statistics are up to date, being based chiefly on 1970 Census data. However, the argument that per capita aid is lower for central cities than for their suburbs even though per capita expenditures are higher is not new. The authors studied the problem intensively for the New York Conference of Mayors and Village Officials in 1969, using 1966-67 data supplied by state agencies to examine expenditure and aid figures for the state's six largest cities. In addition, the Advisory Commission on Intergovernmental Relations in 1967 published a report on *Metropolitan Fiscal*

TABLE 4.11

Central City/Outside Central City Ratios for Expenditures, Taxes, and Intergovernmental Aid, 1970
(37 largest SMSA's in descending order of expenditure ratio)

SMSA	Per Capita Expenditure, CC/OCC	Per Capita Tax Burden, CC/OCC	Intergovern- mental Aid, CC/OCC
Cincinnati	291	187	222
Washington, D.C.	237	223	303
Baltimore	183	113	259
Atlanta	176	207	102
Newark	167	120	271
Denver	164	151	159
St. Louis	159	153	119
Philadelphia	152	139	152
Portland	148	170	123
Providence-Pawtucket-Warwick	148	119	156
Pittsburgh	146	183	117
Boston	146	140	307
Kansas City	140	161	90
Cleveland	139	129	132
New York	139	108	178
Chicago	138	97	170
Columbus (Ohio)	137	122	97
San Francisco-Oakland	129	143	148
Tampa-St. Petersburg	129	179	110
Rochester	127	113	99
Dallas	126	197	77
Miami	124	138	106
San Bernardino-Riverside-Ontario	122	102	129
Los Angeles-Long Beach	118	121	92
Indianapolis	116	150	91
Milwaukee	116	171	89
Seattle-Everett	111	125	85
Anaheim-Santa Ana-Garden Grove	110	94	94
Minneapolis-St. Paul	104	149	78
New Orleans	103	159	86
Detroit	103	121	144
San Diego	103	104	96
Buffalo	102	99	92
Houston	99	105	84
Phoenix	97	114	58
Paterson-Clifton-Passaic	91	79	234
San Jose	90	84	101

SOURCE: Calculated from data in Seymour Sacks and John Callahan, "Central City Suburban Fiscal Disparity," in ACIR, *City Financial Emergencies: The Intergovernmental Dimension* (Washington, D.C., 1973), Tables B-14, B-18, B-23, and B-24, pp. 123, 128, 137–40.

Disparities that reached much the same conclusions.[11] One of its tables, based on 1964-65 data, is reproduced in modified form here as Table 4.12. Note that all the CC/OCC ratios were adverse to central cities at that time except educational expenditures and intergovernmental aid. (The school situation in 1970 was explained earlier in this chapter.) Although intergovernmental aid was the same for cities as for their suburbs on a per capita basis, it was inferior in the cities when expressed as a percentage of both taxes and general operating expenditures.

TABLE 4.12

Summary of Fiscal Disparities Inside and Outside Central Cities, 1964–65
(37 largest SMSA's, unweighted averages)

	CC	OCC	CC/OCC
Per capita total general expenditures	$ 304	$ 265	115
Per capita educational expenditures	99	141	70
Per pupil current expenditures	449	573	78
Per capita general noneducational expenditures	205	124	165
Per capita total general revenue	301	253	119
Per capita taxes	173	137	126
Per capita income	2,482	2,552	97
Per capita federal and state aid	78	78	100
Percentage of general expenditures	25.7%	29.4%	87
Percentage of taxes	45.1%	56.9%	79

SOURCE: Adapted from ACIR, *Fiscal Balance in the American Federal System,* Vol. 2, *Metropolitan Fiscal Disparities* (Washington, D.C., 1967), p. 86.

Changes Occurring in Fiscal Relationships: What of the Future?

Some have looked to the construction of commercial and industrial property to save CC's, since this type of real estate traditionally has been more important there than in the predomi-

nantly residential suburbs. But the recent trend in most SMSA's is
toward the more rapid growth of such buildings outside the central
cities than within. This shifts the tax base differential toward the
suburbs again, easing their fiscal difficulties but not the much
greater ones of the central cities.

A study of the gross assessed values of property[12] in the 27 large
cities and their suburbs for the period 1961-66 shows that the
assessed values rose more rapidly in the OCC areas than in CC's in
every SMSA except New York and Los Angeles, the former because
of an office-building boom and the latter because its very large size
has provided considerable room for expansion within city boundaries. "The property tax base actually declined in Buffalo, Rochester, Cleveland, and Portland while, except in the latter, their
surrounding jurisdictions experienced substantial increases."[13]

The ACIR analysis also shows an actual increase of 25 percent in
median property tax rates for 1957-65 among the central cities of
the 36 largest SMSA's. The range was from 1.4 percent in Louisville and 8 percent in Atlanta to 53 percent in Boston and 50
percent in St. Louis.

Some changes in the CC/OCC ratios from 1960 to 1970 reveal
the bases not only for fiscal disparities between cities and suburbs
but also for the income-expenditure difficulties of central cities.
The first is CC population as a percentage of total SMSA population. It declined from an average of 48 percent to 43 percent for the
72 largest SMSA's and would have fallen further but for annexations. The decrease was particularly noticeable in the Northeast,
where the population ratio fell by one-fifth. As noted above this
means for the central cities both an increase in services to be
performed for suburbanites and a decrease in the relative, if not
absolute, tax base.

Another expense shift indicator is the percentage of nonwhites
and of the elderly. For the 72 largest SMSA's, 86 percent of the
growth in nonwhite populations during the sixties occurred in the central cities and only 14 percent in OCC areas. The
percentage of people over age 65 went up 11 percent in CC's as
compared with only 8 percent outside.

On the ability-to-pay side of the picture, median family incomes in CC's rose only 19 percent from 1959 to 1968, while in suburbia they went up 27 percent.

Per capita total expenditures for the 37 largest SMSA's went up 180 percent in central cities between 1957 and 1970, compared with only 140 percent outside central cities (weighted average). For per capita taxes, however, the rates of increase were reversed: 120 percent for central cities and 140 percent for suburban areas outside central cities. This is an indication of the way the fiscal plight of central cities has been recognized by state and federal governments through intergovernmental aid programs. State and local aid per capita went up 370 percent for CC's during this interval as compared with only 210 percent for OCC's.

We believe that most of these trends will continue. The regional differences also will remain, but increasingly the cities of the far West and South will experience the same problems that have beset the older northeastern cities in recent decades. The younger cities, as they grow and age, will lose industry and upper income population to their own suburbs and will only partly offset these losses by urban renewal efforts, financed largely by the Federal government. Fiscal tensions will mount. The trend toward their relief by intergovernmental aid, however, is not so certain.

General revenue sharing modeled on the 1972 legislation does not seem to focus on urban fiscal need as much as many of the categorical grant programs.[14] Therefore, while federal revenue sharing will help recipients in general, central cities may not be differentially favored by it. Figures released for the Albany-Schenectady-Troy metropolitan area reveal the three central cities getting only about one-fourth of the federal funds distributed as payments in this SMSA for the first half of 1972. On a per capita basis the CC area got $4.80 as opposed to $7.30 for the OCC part of the SMSA. If this is representative of the country as a whole, a lot of central city mayors and taxpayers are going to be unhappy, particularly since their allotments are generally lower than at first predicted when 1967 figures were used in the formula instead of the 1971 data that later became available.

An editorial called "The Forgotten Cities," which appeared in
The New York Times on December 10,1972, the day following
announcement of the new allocations, supports the above conjec-
ture and neatly summarizes the whole city-versus-suburb dilemma, albeit from the viewpoint of the central city:

When Federal revenue sharing was still only a political dream
of tax money flowing back to the area of greatest need, urban
reformers were convinced that the hardpressed cities would reap
the greatest benefits. It was not an unreasonable hope. The
details of the "urban crisis" had been spelled out for years at
every political symposium. The extent of that crisis was unmistakeable to anyone who had ever walked through inner-city
slums or had measured the escalating costs of urban government
for education, welfare, housing and policing.

But now that the small print of the prospective revenue-
sharing allocations has become available, the nature of the urban
crisis appears once again to have been overlooked. The Federal
Government may have arrived at its system of allocations by way
of a logic different from that of the state legislatures which have
so long short-changed the cities, but the ultimate effect is
unfortunately destined to be not substantially different.

New York City's share, for example, is to be 20 percent less
than the amounts that had originally been projected by the
Treasury Department when Congress was drawing up the plan.
Most of New York's and New Jersey's big cities—and presumably cities throughout the country—will be similarly affected.

The explanation offered in Washington is that the shared
revenue slices are being adjusted in the light of recent population growth. This means that the expanding suburbs will
benefit, while the more static, older communities will lose out.

This is a triumph of statistics over socioeconomic facts. The
cities are in trouble because they are old and relatively static.
Their capital equipment, suffering from age, is more costly to
maintain and in need of replacement. Suburban growth is
largely the result of the influx of the more affluent population

sector that leaves the cities. The urban population is therefore not only static but disproportionately poor. It is in need of more expensive services as the only hope of being liberated from the unproductive and costly condition of poverty.

Any revenue-sharing formula that penalizes urban areas for being static and old can only have the effect of abandoning the cities to decay. A realistic and imaginative approach to the return of tax revenues to the states and localities would be to give special consideration to the high cost of urban rebirth.

The present formula is symptomatic of a society that thoughtlessly and wastefully believes that the superficial vitality of the suburban sprawl alone is sufficient insurance of economic growth and societal health. In reality, the cities cannot safely be treated as superannuated pensioners. Suburban growth around dying cities is the prelude to suburban deterioration as well. The cities are the centers that must be made to hold. Revenue sharing, to be effective, will have to write that goal into its formula.

Notes

1 Jane Jacobs, *The Economy of Cities* (New York: Random House, 1969).
2 U.S. Senate Select Committee on Nutrition and Human Needs, *Hunger 1973,* 1973, p. 3.
3 David L. Birch, *The Economic Future of City and Suburb* (New York: Committee for Economic Development, 1970).
4 Generally speaking an SMSA consists of a county or group of counties containing at least one city or twin cities having a population of 50,000 or more plus adjacent counties that are metropolitan in character and are economically and socially integrated with the central city (which is defined as the largest city in the SMSA). In New England, towns and cities rather than counties are the units used in defining SMSA's. The name of the central city is used as the name of the SMSA. There is no limit to the number of adjacent counties included in SMSA so long as they are integrated with the Central City nor is an SMSA limited to a single state. In an SMSA, the area within a Central City is referred to as "inside central city" and the rest is called "outside central city." In 1969, there were 233 SMSA's in

the United States. (See U.S.
Bureau of the Census, *1970 Census
User's Guide, Part I,* p. 79.)

5 Birch, *op. cit.,* pp. 29-32.

6 Edward C. Banfield, *The Unheavenly City* (Boston: Little,
Brown, 1970), Ch. 2.

7 Birch, *op. cit.,* p. 24.

8 Technically the ratio would be
1.00, not 100, but we follow
ACIR and other authors in calling
a percentage figure a ratio.

9 Woo Kee, "City-Suburb Differentials in Local Government Fiscal
Effort," *National Tax Journal,* Vol.
21, June 1968.

10 Seymour Sacks and John Callahan,
"Central City Suburban Fiscal
Disparity," in ACIR, *City Financial Emergencies: The Intergovernmental Dimension* (Washington, D.C.,
1973), pp. 91-152.

11 Robert B. Pettengill, Kuan-I
Chen, and J. S. Uppal, *Cities and
Suburbs: The Case for Equity, Part I.
State Aid to Big Cities in New York
State and to Their Suburbs* (Albany,
New York: New York Conference
of Mayors and Village Officials,
1970); and ACIR, *Fiscal Balance in
the American Federal System,* Vol. 2,
Metropolitan Fiscal Disparities
(Washington, D.C., 1967), p.
86. We note some differences between the figures presented by the
ACIR and those that may be calculated from the statistics in U.S.
Bureau of the Census, *City Government Finances,* 1971-72, but we
understand that the apparent dis-
crepancies are due to the fact that
the ACIR data include amounts for
appropriate overlapping political
jurisdictions.

12 At least half the states have partial
exemptions from the local general
property tax, such as those for
homesteads, veterans, and senior
citizens; but these amount to less
than 5 percent of the total gross
valuation. In 1966, for instance,
the total gross assessed valuation of
property subject to local general
property taxes was $499.0 billion.
Subtracting the exemptions noted
above, reduced the "net assessed
valuation" to $484.1 billion.
Government holdings, church
properties, and the like are also
exempt from taxation, but their
value is not included in the gross
assessed valuation figure. (See
U.S. Department of Commerce,
*Trends in Assessed Valuations and
Sales Ratios, 1956-66.,* March,
1970, p. 1.)

13 ACIR, *Fiscal Balance in the American Federal System,* op. cit., pp.
82-91.

14 See Chapter 5 for further discussion of this point.

5

CONFLICT

AND

COMPROMISE

The Human Condition

Groups of people are very much like the individuals who make up the aggregates. As Plato said, "The State is man writ large." To him this meant the city-state, so we are not stretching his meaning if we say that cities have much the same problems and seek many of the same temporary solutions as does each of us. Among these problems are fiscal ones, and here the analogy seems particularly apt. Men and cities have wants that exceed their capacities to satisfy. Some satisfactions must always be foregone. Even when maintaining a given level of living with customary income, choices must be made.

These decisions become more difficult to make when income falls or desires rise. We become more conscious of what we have to give up to get what we want, more aware of "opportunity costs." If our plight is caused by inflation, if the prices of goods and services in our budgets have risen, we cannot buy as much as before with the same income. The painful decision must be made whether to cut down on this item or that. Now the academic question becomes real, how to distinguish between "necessities" and "luxuries" in deciding what to forego. Furthermore, cities, like families, are made up of people with different priorities, different value judgments to reconcile or compromise. There is no longer a relatively simple case of substitution at the margin, but a tug of war in which the desires of the strong prevail over those of the weak. The satisfactions of one group may be obtained by imposing costs on another.

The big taxpayers of a city usually dominate urban fiscal policy, whether a single firm provides the largest chunk of property tax revenue or whether a group of firms is organized into a powerful industrial council or chamber of commerce. At other times homeowners may form an association and speak with a loud voice at City Hall, especially against any increase in the property tax, which they usually see as more menacing than the sales tax chiefly because it takes such big bites on the days when it must be paid.[1] Or, as Saul Alinsky demonstrated,[2] city minority or low-income groups may become conscious of their potential power on election day and, organizing, wield it successfully.

As in family fiscal crises, urban budget decisions are dictated by custom, by vested interests, by whoever wields the power. An outsider may not be able to perceive much "rationality" in decisions about how to deal with revenue-expenditure tensions. But whether a decision is properly called rational or not depends, we argue, upon one's knowledge of facts, upon perceptions of relevant functions linking variables, and upon value priorities. Since these are essentially subjective, those who pass judgments about other people's choices need to make very clear their own assumptions about rationality.

No city ever completely solves its fiscal crisis in the sense of putting an end to it. What happens is that the painful choice is made for one year's budget, and the agony of decision-making is then over for another twelve months. In this respect cities do not differ significantly from other governmental units. The costs of government are rising at all levels, and additional services are everywhere in demand, just like the problems of a growing family whose children are needing more and more as they get older. School districts, states, and the federal government itself have annual "crises" at budget time resembling those of the cities. They all have similar options and must choose among similar alternatives, except that the federal government cannot look upward for aid.[3]

Predicting Future Crises: The Revenue Gap

If things look bad in our cities today, what will they be like tomorrow? A number of competent studies show that urban expenditures are growing more rapidly than tax revenues at existing rates. Most of these have focused on states or on state and local governments grouped together, but their findings indicate the nature of the urban problem if not its precise dimensions. For instance, Mushkin, Lupo, and Friedman, in a report prepared for the Joint Economic Committee of the Congress,[3] show state and local tax revenues increasing at approximately the same rate as the GNP, an income elasticity of 1.0, but expenditures rising at a multiple of 1.6 or 1.7. A similar study for states alone by the Advisory Commission for Intergovernmental Relations[4] shows a general revenue elasticity of 0.9 and general expenditure elasticity of 1.7. Other studies by Netzer, Tax Foundation Project 70, and the Committee for Economic Development show growth disparities of approximately the same magnitudes.[5]

This is the source of the persistent crises of the past and the inevitable tension of the future. The Weintraub TEMPO study for the National League of Cities tried to dramatize the problem by quantifying a "revenue gap" for U.S. cities in each year of a 10-year period, 1965-75. Adding the annual amounts, he came up with a $262 billion revenue deficiency for the decade. (See Table 5.1.) Even if we don't protest his using an 11 percent annual increment for expenditures, higher than the usual estimates cited, against a 6.5 percent rate of increase for revenues from own sources and intergovernmental aid combined, one may still question the logic of computing an aggregate gap of this magnitude. In practice, the gap is closed each year in one way or another as cities start afresh.

The TEMPO team clearly exaggerated in its effort to make a
generally accepted point: cities need more revenue and must find
ways to get it if expenditures are not to be cut.

TABLE 5.1

Weintraub's Estimated Annual Gaps Between City Government
Revenue Needs and Expectations
(In billions)

Fiscal Year	(1) Expenditures	(2) Revenues from Own Sources	(3) Intergovern- mental Aid	(4) Revenue Gaps (1) — (2) + (3)
1966	$ 61.0	$ 40.2	$ 16.3	$ 4.5
1967	68.0	42.7	17.4	7.9
1968	76.0	45.4	18.6	12.0
1969	85.0	48.4	19.9	16.7
1970	95.0	51.5	21.3	22.2
1971	106.0	54.7	22.8	28.5
1972	117.0	58.1	24.4	34.5
1973	128.0	61.8	26.1	40.1
1974	139.0	65.7	27.9	45.4
1975	150.0	69.8	29.9	50.3
10-Year Totals	$1,025.0	$538.3	$224.6	$262.1

SOURCE: Robert E. Weintraub, *Options for Meeting the Revenue Needs of
City Governments* (Santa Barbara, Calif.: TEMPO, General Electric Company, 1967), p. 6.

In 1972 an amazingly different type of projection appeared.
This study by the American Enterprise Institute predicted for
cities (and states) that a surplus instead of a deficit would prevail in
the years ahead. Unfortunately, it does not show clearly how its
projections were calculated. It merely says that expenditure estimates were:

built around two demographic variables, the projected number

of students enrolled in public education at all levels and projected population. In addition, a "quality adjustment" is built
in—that is, allowance is made for the trend rate of increase since
1954 in *real* state and local education expenditures per pupil and
real per capita expenditures for other purposes.[6]

Elsewhere the authors of this study indicate that they think state
and local expenditures will increase less rapidly in the future than
in the past because of the end of the period of "soaring school
enrollments" and "rapid family formation." The authors do not
explain their revenue projections very well either, but refer only to
general revenue sharing and "a new welfare program" in the Nixon
budget. They also cite the record to show that an actual surplus
emerged in 1970-72 and imply that this indicates that "pressures
on total state and local spending may well be abating." As a result,
they conclude, "the federal government may be in the process of
beggaring itself to relieve many state and local governments from
having to finance outlays that may never be needed. . . ."[7]

The press interpreted the AEI study as questioning the need for
federal revenue sharing. What it actually shows (in regard to the
1970-72 surplus) is that a cyclical upturn in business raises tax
revenues. Also, some state and local governments apparently had
not yet budgeted adequately for the growing intergovernmental
grants-in-aid already on their way. Acting conservatively, their
budgets had not raised expenditures or reduced taxes as rapidly as
they could have done. More of both will be possible in the future as
the $6 billion annually from federal general revenue sharing is
distributed. Cities that have been cutting expenditures will be able
to rehire people laid off, restore welfare payments to earlier levels,
improve health standards, and so on. Property taxpayers may be
relieved of some of their burden, but a more logical prediction is
that they will not get a very big slice of the melon. Spending needs
are just too great and there also seem to be a lot of pet projects of
mayors and city councilmen like new parks, city halls, municipal
auditoriums, and other capital improvements, not to mention
salary increases for the faithful.

The upward trend of government costs is inexorable. If there are fewer children in public schools in the future, the trend is more likely to be toward smaller classes than to fewer teachers, and school pay scales are rising. Even the declining public school enrollment prediction may be exaggerated in the light of the accelerating closures of parochial schools (413 in 1971). Parochiaid devices, even if some are found to be constitutional, are unlikely to keep many church schools open, and their expense means either more taxes for some people or cuts in the budgets of our public schools. Without all present federal aid, and more, it seems very unlikely that the state and local sector will be, as the AEI predicts, "in a position to slow down tax increases or actually cut taxes and still provide improved services for most citizens." The Senate Subcommittee on Intergovernmental Relations found out in its November 1972 survey that the "vast majority of cities—both large and small—intended to spend on capital improvements, including streets and roads; public safety; and salary adjustments, including hiring new personnel. Somewhat less frequently mentioned were various forms of tax relief and environment improvements."[8]

There remains to be considered the quantitative question of whether urban expenditures per capita are likely to rise more slowly in the future. The Tax Foundation thinks so.[9] In 1972 reduced urban needs were perceived by some as the result of declining unemployment (clearly cyclical), a slower rate of population growth (hopefully secular), a passing of the post World War II baby boom bulge in the demand for K-12 schooling, and the influence of conservative national leadership stressing self-reliance and reduced spending on public services like welfare (surely part of a political cycle of uncertain length.)

In a recent (1973) study, the Tax Foundation, on the basis of forecasts of revenues and expenditures of state and local governments, has projected surpluses during 1975 and 1980. The existence of surpluses, however, does not prove that needs are being adequately met. It is interesting to note that in its otherwise optimistic forecast, the Tax Foundation makes a pessimistic observation about the future of the American cities. Commenting on the financial future of local governments in general, the Tax Foundation has remarked, "There are needs not being met, and acute fiscal problems in some areas, particularly in some large and old cities. How to solve these 'pocket' problems within our present intergovernmental revenue system, despite years of discussion, still remains something of an enigma."[10]

If these downturns in per capita spending are not just wishful thinking, their coming should already be casting its shadow before. But Table 5.2 and Figure 5.1, which present data on recent spending trends, do not support the fiscal optimists. Expenses are rising in every category, far exceeding the general rate of inflation, which was about 60 percent from 1955 to 1972.

Table 5.2 and Figure 5.1 deal only with major items in present budgets. Also looming on the horizon for anyone to see are the mounting nimbus clouds of pollution control expenses, rising energy costs, and the not unrelated needs for expensive urban mass transit. These seem appropriately labeled "needs" even if improvements in urban housing and education are relegated to the status of mere "wants." Rising general levels of living are also predictable, and with them will surely come demands for more adequate subsistence budgets for the nonworking urban poor. If we put all these together as foreseeable future demands for greater urban spending, a falling barometer looks more likely than fair weather.

First Alternative: Raise More Revenue From Own Sources

Cities that want to spend more presumably must try to raise more revenue at home[11] But how? It's easier said than done. There is no painless way, but some methods are less painful than others.

The degree of pain has to be appraised both politically and economically. In the present frame of reference, economic pain in the short run might be considered the reduction in the level of living forced upon those who have to pay more taxes or charges to

TABLE 5.2

Per Capita City General Expenditure Trends by Categories, 1955–72

Year	Education	Highways	Public Welfare	Health and Hospitals	Police and Fire	Sewers and Sanitation	Housing and Urban Renewal
1955	$12.03	$11.63	$ 4.90	$ 6.00	$15.50	$10.00	$ 2.10
1960	15.52	13.56	5.24	6.88	18.62	11.48	4.00
1965	21.39	15.53	7.97	9.59	24.79	15.24	5.89
1972	44.14	20.97	22.96	21.00	46.59	24.99	11.17

NOTE: Figures include capital expenditures that were excluded in Tables 2.2 and 2.3. The 1972 figures are for the fiscal year.

SOURCE: U.S. Bureau of the Census, City Government Finances, for various years.

FIGURE 5.1

Rise in Per Capita Spending for All Cities, by Categories, 1955–72

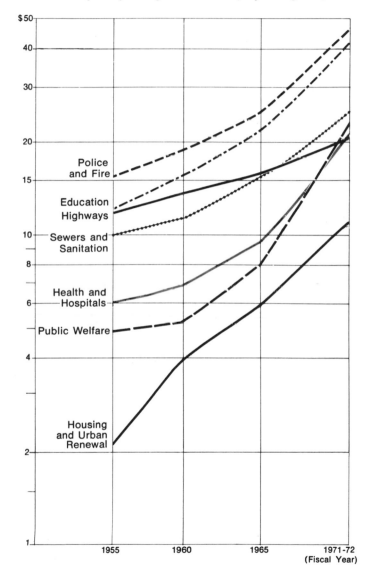

provide cities with additional revenues. In the long run, economic pain includes also any erosion of the tax base. However, as suggested earlier, long-run considerations of this type rarely carry much weight in the preparation of annual budgets. That is where the political pain comes in. A large part of the urban fiscal crisis may be viewed as the way in which additions to the tax bill jeopardize the reelection of those who propose the increases. Economic pain becomes political pain when powerful toes kick against those who step in the wrong place. The dilemma of the budget makers is how to choose between one set of toes and another, for someone's foot must be stepped on.

Another problem arises from interregional competition for taxpayers. Other things being equal, they tend to locate where taxes are lowest. If taxes in one city rise too much above those in nearby communities, people tend to move out to a lower-taxed suburb. So do business firms. It is akin to the way in which rising wage rates in the North have stimulated firms to relocate in the low wage South. The effort to get more golden eggs drives away the taxpaying geese.

To avoid this long-run misfortune, some argue that expenditures should be cut or held at their present level. But that, too, is painful to those denied services or to employees laid off from shrinking city department payrolls. Deterioration of services also pushes people out to the suburbs. Caught on the horns of this particular dilemma, city administrations usually choose the one with the least immediate pain and keep their fingers crossed about the long run.

On closer examination the above statement of alternatives is perceived as oversimplifying the problem. There are not just two or three choices to be made; there are many. And most options are not mutually exclusive. We may choose some of each. That means quantitative decisions, or balancing additions and subtractions to get approximate equality at the margin. There are different types of tax from which to choose, each with myriad rate possibilities, different forms of fiscal federalism, different ways of getting varying amounts of intergovernmental aid, and a host of different cuts that could be made in expenditure budgets. There is also more than one goal to be considered. Justice and human values must not be overlooked in the efforts to reduce fiscal tensions and achieve political viability.

UNDERUTILIZED REVENUE SOURCES FOR CITIES

Most cities are constrained in their ability to solve their fiscal difficulties by their own action as a result of state imposed restrictions upon them. Wanting to raise property taxes, cities in 17 states are held back by provisions of their state constitutions. Twenty-two more states require time-consuming and uncertain local referenda, special state legislation, and the like before city property taxes may exceed certain limits. In only 11 states do cities have the independent right to unlimited property tax increases.

If cities in a bind try to turn to other forms of taxation to gain relief, they may find even higher hurdles, some of them constitutional, some statutory. States themselves now rely much more on the sales tax than on the property tax and are increasingly (in 40 states) using the income tax. That is one reason why only 6 states now give cities unlimited use of the sales tax and none grants that freedom for the income tax. Where some adoption is allowed, top limits for rates are carefully specified. Special legislation may be required to initiate or to raise the rates of either of these taxes. Sometimes this has led to adjacent cities having different rates with the lower-ceiling city protesting its inability to tax as heavily as its neighbor.

Table 5.3 presents recent data for 48 large cities showing how infrequently the sales and income taxes are used and how little these taxes usually amount to as a percentage of revenues raised internally. They seem clearly underutilized.

DIFFICULTIES IN CITY USE OF THE PROPERTY
TAX TO RAISE MORE REVENUES

When cities need more money in the future, they will get much of it from the general property tax. They have done so in the past (see Chapter 3), and we see no reason to doubt that they will

TABLE 5.3

Utilization of Nonproperty Taxes by 48 Largest Cities, 1970–71

City	Sales Tax Revenue		Income Tax Revenue		All Nonproperty Taxes	
	Per Capita	Percentage Own Resources	Per Capita	Percentage Own Resources	Per Capita	Percentage Own Resources
Atlanta	—	—	—	—	$ 40.73	21.68%
Baltimore	—	—	$ 34.20	11.50%	60.16	20.20
Birmingham	$ 23.90	21.3%	—	—	49.11	43.80
Boston	—	—	—	—	5.10	1.10
Buffalo	12.47	5.8	—	—	19.20	8.89
Chicago	19.66	12.0	—	—	52.04	36.39
Cincinnati	—	—	62.70	17.17	70.92	19.40
Cleveland	—	—	55.20	29.14	59.33	31.31
Columbus	—	—	59.80	47.51	63.88	50.69
Dallas	25.5	13.1	—	—	38.66	24.27
Denver	67.37	26.6	—	—	98.42	38.84
Detroit	—	—	58.39	26.99	68.52	31.89
El Paso	13.39	14.1	—	—	19.60	22.67
Fort Worth	20.34	17.5	—	—	26.46	22.71
Honolulu	—	—	—	—	32.49	21.02
Houston	23.18	19.4	—	—	33.47	28.01

City	Sales Tax Revenue		Income Tax Revenue		All Nonproperty Taxes	
	Per Capita	Percentage Own Resources	Per Capita	Percentage Own Resources	Per Capita	Percentage Own Resources
Indianapolis	—	—	—	—	1.26	1.07
Jacksonville	—	—	—	—	32.92	24.57
Kansas City	—	—	31.23	16.43	77.86	43.41
Long Beach	20.87	9.4	—	—	43.59	20.08
Los Angeles	23.45	13.4	—	—	56.55	32.35
Louisville	—	—	54.93	31.91	61.95	37.14
Memphis	—	—	—	—	24.43	15.52
Miami	—	—	—	—	42.61	28.56
Milwaukee	—	—	—	—	3.42	2.26
Minneapolis	—	—	—	—	11.97	7.94
Nashville-Davison	40.96	16.3	—	—	63.03	25.07
Newark	—	—	—	—	29.55	9.23
New Orleans	44.43	26.7	—	—	66.83	40.16
New York City	62.52	12.5	56.96	11.36	158.49	31.61
Norfolk	19.41	8.0	—	—	81.81	33.66
Oakland	26.25	13.0	—	—	48.34	24.63
Oklahoma City	27.47	22.0	—	—	36.47	29.49
Omaha	13.87	12.8	—	—	25.42	24.04
Philadelphia	—	—	116.06	46.79	133.53	53.58
Phoenix	29.83	26.0	—	—	51.32	45.00

(continued on next page)

TABLE 5.3 (continued)

City	Sales Tax Revenue		Income Tax Revenue		All Nonproperty Taxes	
	Per Capita	Percentage Own Resources	Per Capita	Percentage Own Resources	Per Capita	Percentage Own Resources
Pittsburgh	—	—	25.50	15.39	60.16	36.32
Portland	—	—	—	—	19.67	14.24
St. Louis	14.04	6.1	59.34	25.86	120.75	52.29
St. Paul	—	—	—	—	18.34	14.06
San Antonio	13.72	16.8	—	—	16.60	19.50
San Diego	21.21	16.7	—	—	32.03	25.23
San Francisco	43.14	8.9	12.01	2.5	79.88	18.00
San Jose	19.64	15.1	—	—	36.61	28.14
Seattle	9.61	5.3	—	—	54.89	30.39
Toledo	—	—	60.70	50.70	63.84	53.33
Tulsa	24.95	21.7	—	—	32.41	28.0
Washington, D.C.	102.60	15.5	172.10	26.31	395.00	59.77
Average of 48 cities	24.74	9.51	28.39	10.92	79.84	30.70

SOURCE: U.S. Bureau of the Census, City Government Finances, 1970–71.

continue to do so in the years ahead. Real property is highly visible, highly immobile, and highly esteemed as a measure of wealth, even in Bazelon's paper economy.[12] Tradition hallows the property tax. It has long been the mainstay of local governments and property owners have become somewhat inured to their annual tax bills. "There's nothing more certain than death and taxes" is an old saying that grew out of many centuries of reliance upon the property tax. The question is really not whether city real estate taxes will rise but how much, and with what modifications in the tax pattern.

Even so, the increased revenues will not be obtained easily. Cries of protest against the property tax are getting louder, as shown by the increasingly frequent defeats of municipal bond issues and school budgets.[13] For instance, at the November 1972 elections Detroit voters for the third time refused to approve a renewal of a special 5 mill property tax ($5 for every $1,000 assessed valuation) intended for the school system. Facing an $80 million deficit, the city Board of Education voted to close the 300 public schools for seven weeks after the Christmas vacation unless new money could be found. The Governor said the state legislature was not likely to help with money, but might pass a law allowing the Detroit City Council to raise city property taxes higher than elsewhere in the state, including, of course, those in Detroit's white suburbs. This it did in early 1973, and the schools weathered the crisis and remained open.

Contributing to the growing tax rebellion probably is the rise in home ownership and the tax consciousness that brings. Before World War II, only 53 percent of American families owned their homes. In 1950, the rate rose to 55 percent; in 1970 it reached 59 percent. Whereas tenants pay a hidden property tax in their monthly rent checks, when they become owners, they pay a very visible, very large lump sum twice a year (except in these cases where a monthly mortgage payment includes taxes). Even the composite mortgage payment may rise visibly once a year because of property tax increases. For these reasons voters are much more conscious of rising property taxes than before. So even if the family income of the average homeowner goes up in the same year, he is apt to begrudge the increase in taxes just as he does increases in grocery prices. Both are inescapable, and both particularly hurt those on small fixed incomes like the aged on pensions or Social Security. Hence if a major tax increase is imposed to finance a substantial rise in projected spending, political incumbents should expect that opposing candidates will find a large audience of home-owning voters receptive to the argument that they are being un-justly treated by city hall. Landlords having difficulty shifting the property tax increases to their tenants are likely to feel the same way.

Resistance to property tax increases sometimes comes from city hall itself, from those who are afraid that higher tax rates will drive more industry and more middle and upper class people out of the city to the suburbs (see Chapter 4). In the short run higher rates produce more revenue, but in the long run they may erode the tax base and force future taxes to rise faster than they otherwise would.

The truth in this argument is often exaggerated, however. It is not all tax rate increases that produce this undesired effect but chiefly the portion in excess of the rise elsewhere. As stated in an earlier chapter, the reasons for business and residential movement are very complex, and tax differentials are surely only one of several factors. Population growth, the aging of buildings, the rise of urban congestion, a decline in the quality of urban services, changes in industrial technology, and even rising affluence itself may be among the paramount forces.[14] Causes differ with cases. The straws on the camel's back are probably more or less inter-changeable, so singling out one as the backbreaking culprit may be very arbitrary.

Another reason why property tax increases are tolerated is that many payers can shift them forward to their customers. This is clearly true of regulated monopolies like electricity producers, telephone companies, and other utilities. These firms are virtually guaranteed a "fair" rate of return by public utility commissions. If property taxes go up, rates are permitted to rise to cover the tax increase. Private firms with substantial monopoly power are in almost the same position. Even those who face strong competition can shift property taxes forward if their rivals are similarly pressured. It is only when rivals in other political jurisdictions have more favorable property tax experience that tax increases hurt and loud protests are heard.

The owners of commercial or residential income property are in a peculiar position when their property taxes rise. Their freedom to shift these increases is limited by the terms of the leases held by their tenants. Long commercial leases may require lessee payment of all property taxes. Others contain escalator clauses to deal with tax boost contingencies. Residential leases usually do not protect landlords in that way and are generally quite short. When they expire, tax shifting power will be high if the nearby vacancy rate is low. If there are many empty apartments, the situation resembles that of business firms in an industry operating far below capacity. Owners don't dare raise rents for fear of competitors' not following suit. At such times they tend to protest tax increases more loudly than usual.

REDUCING DISCRIMINATION AS A METHOD OF DIMINISHING PROPERTY TAX RESISTANCE

Nobody likes to pay taxes, but they are a necessary evil. Tax resistance is heightened if many people feel they are being discriminated against. "No taxation without representation" is a slogan familiar to every American who knows his country's history. "Don't tax me without taxing him" is another complaint. Property tax payers have used this argument with considerable force in cities that did not levy sales and income taxes. But as the use of these and other nonproperty sources of revenue has become more widespread (see Chapter 3), this discrimination ground for opposing higher property tax rates has diminished.

Another form of discrimination arises from the feeling among poor homeowners that the weight of their tax burden exceeds that of the more affluent, a verdict that some of the latter would accept and even join in affirming. To reduce the opposition of this bloc to increases in real estate taxes, the "circuit-breaker" plan was invented, and its use is spreading. Under this device low income

persons, especially the elderly, are relieved of part or all of the
property taxes on their homes, the amount of relief varying in-
versely with income and usually held to a modest statutory ceiling.
Most of the states now using this formula grant a credit toward
income taxes due, but some make a tax rebate. The latter would
seem the best approach for cities, since only a few of them levy
income taxes. Or a direct credit might be granted on the property
tax bill itself upon proper declaration of income from all sources.
People who rent instead of owning their homes are sometimes
given a similar relief on a percentage basis. Twenty-five percent of
total annual rent paid (up to a statutory maximum) seems a
reasonable figure, since for the country as a whole property tax
liabilities on rental dwellings now average about 23 percent of
gross rent. Adjustment of this percentage could be made to fit the
tax patterns of individual cities in a manner comparable to the 10
percent to 30 percent range presently existing among the states.
The "circuit-breaker" plan clearly reduces property tax revenues
but, by also reducing opposition to higher tax rates, may prove a
net gain.

   Another sense of injustice arising from discrimination is related
to an old problem of the property tax, inequitable assessments.
When some people feel they are being taxed more heavily than
their neighbors or people like them in other cities, they protest
property tax increases more loudly than they otherwise would do.
Uneven assessment of real property arises either from rules that
favor one class of property over another or from inefficiency or
favoritism in the assessment process itself.

   Residential property for instance may be assessed as a matter of
policy at a lower fraction of true market value than is business
property, presumably on the grounds that the businessman can
shift most or all of his taxes to his customers, while homeowners
cannot. Their tax burden is real and inescapable. The practice of
assessing unimproved land in cities at the lowest percentage of all
relative to market value perhaps derives from its nonproduction of
income, either monetary as with business or service as with the
homeowner. This reasoning, of course, is the opposite of that of the

Single Taxer, who would demand that it pay heavy taxes just because it is not producing anything of value, except a potential future capital gain for its owner.

Nine states now designate several classes of property and stipulate the different assessment ratios that are to be used for each class. In most states, however, a uniform ratio is mandated for all property. Violations of the uniformity rule are so widespread, however, that inequities abound and are hard to terminate. People illegally getting the advantage of a 40 percent assessment in a 100 percent state find it hard to protest very loudly about their neighbor getting twice as good a deal at 20 percent. But if there were a classified assessment group for single-family homes at 30 percent, he would feel free to complain to the assessor. Now all he can do is to protest the present level of, and any increases in, property tax rates. The same would hold true for commercial properties whose norm might be set much higher.

Assessors, too, would have better grounds for resisting pressures for discriminatory favoritism. When every home is assessed below the 100 percent figure prescribed by law, how far below becomes a matter of discretion or of persuasion. A uniform class rule at 20 percent or 30 percent would give a realizable norm for correcting inequities in either direction. It would also encourage periodic reassessments of all pieces of property in that class, a task infrequently attempted for all property in a city because the huge staff required and the expense involved would be utterly beyond the capacity of the usual assessor's office.

Piecemeal reassessment is almost inevitably capricious and provokes more resentment than gratitude. Yet this method is the rule rather than the exception. Understaffed assessors usually reduce assessments only when there is strong complaint, either vehemence or persistence on the part of the small guy or implied threats by the big. Increases are made only when particular pieces of property are sold at prices substantially higher than the values used to determine the prior assessment figure. During a period of rising land values caused by general price inflation and population growth, people who hold on to property acquired many years earlier get a tax advantage over recent purchasers. Of course the opposite trend can also occur in some cities or parts of cities, but it is relatively rare in a country like ours where price inflation is pretty general, population is growing, and industries expand.

Discrimination also arises when income property is valued by formulae that may be interpreted or twisted in different ways. Even if improvements are valued at cost less depreciation according to a certain rule of accounting, there are ways to deflate apparent original cost and to claim faster depreciation. But capitalization of income is the method that offers the greatest opportunities for discrimination, unintentional or otherwise. Owners of a new building, for instance, may ask for a valuation of the structure for tax purposes considerably below their construction cost on the ground that the property was overbuilt and rents will not yield a reasonable return on the investment. Or at a later date when net income falls for fortuitous, cyclical, or competitive reasons, requests for downward revaluations may be granted. Prospective earnings figured for tax appeal purposes will be predicted as pessimistically as possible, and tax assessors usually do not have staff with the time or ability needed to challenge the red ink figures presented by large corporate taxpayers. Of course, when Lady Luck is more favorable and incomes rise above expectations, there is rarely any demand for higher valuations.

Formula flexibility really works both ways. To the extent that it reduces a sense of injustice by those whose misfortune prompts a successful request for tax relief, it helps to preserve the property tax. Others who are also pinched but get no relief may feel discriminated against and protest tax rate increases, which hurt them more than ever.

One more case of discrimination under the property tax is the way in which personal property is frequently taxed at a lower rate than real property and some forms escape taxation entirely. One might argue in defense of such discrimination that owners of capital claims (e.g., stocks, bonds, notes, savings accounts, etc.) cannot shift their taxes forward the way most owners of real property and tangible personalty are able to do. Nor can owners of non-income-producing personalty like home furnishings, jewelry, and checking accounts. In other words, they are like homeowners, but if the latter are taxed on the grounds that they own wealth, why not the former, and at the same rate?

REFORMS DESIGNED TO PRODUCE MORE REVENUE

This suggests an obvious way for cities to increase the revenue raised by the general property tax: include personalty in the tax base and tax it at the same rate as realty. The problems are those of discovery and the sense of injustice if the honest who declare their concealable assets get taxed while the dishonest escape. Granted that concealment will long thwart tax collectors, when we reach the day of universal computer information data banks, most capital claims presumably will be recorded at the time of origin and the change in ownership noted with every subsequent transfer. Taxing authorities would not then have to depend on the honesty of the holders of these property rights and could tax them, if they chose, just like the tangible property that now bears 90 percent of the property tax burden.

The federal government now requires corporate payers of interest and dividends to report to the Bureau of Internal Revenue all payee names and amounts as a way of checking up on possible concealment of income subject to the personal income tax. If the courts permit this disclosure in order to help Uncle Sam raise revenue, why not do the same to help the hard-pressed cities? Internal Revenue offices have the addresses of all these payees, and it would be easy to write computer programs that separated them by location as a basis for supplying city assessors with information about who owned income-producing securities that should be declared as wealth subject to tax. Such a move would raise cries of invasion of privacy, but why should the owners of personalty be given a veil of secrecy that is denied to real property owners by the custom of permitting full access to the books in city and county assessors' officers? Bank deposit secrecy laws would be harder to surmount, but the inequity argument that some concealment of wealth would still be possible should not block cities from action to reduce inequity and gain a much needed additional revenue source.

In the preceding section of this chapter the uneven assessment of real property was criticized for the way in which its perceived injustice tends to obstruct increases in property tax rates. More important is the way in which it holds down the size of the tax base. To the extent that inefficiency or favoritism causes some properties on the tax rolls to be assessed at a lower ratio to market value than others in their group, the cities are denied revenue that they should claim and receive. The remedy is not difficult if city councils are willing to endure the cries of anguish from those whose assessment is raised. Either hire impartial outside assessing firms to do the job, shift the responsibility to a better financed higher level of government, or expand the staff of existing assessors' offices to permit more thorough and more frequent reassessment across the board. Netzer estimates that good assessment might cost 1.5 percent of tax collections annually,[15] but this would surely be much less than the gains from upward valuation of now-favored property.

Even with professional and unbiased assessment, some inequities would remain. According to Netzer, even in "good" assessment cities and states, the *average* deviation from the median assessment ratios can be large by equity standards. Only one of the 1,356 areas examined in the 1962 U. S. *Census of Governments* had a deviation for single-family homes of as low as 5 percent, and only 8 others were below 10 percent. Fully half the areas, including six large cities—New York, Chicago, St. Louis, Boston, San Francisco, and Minneapolis—all able to afford good assessment staffs if they want them, showed a coefficient of dispersion[16] of more than 30 percent. Several other major cities, including Detroit and Philadelphia, were in the 20-30 percent range, along with a quarter of the rest of the sample. Los Angeles, Cleveland, and Washington, D.C., were in the one-fifth of the group in the less than 20 percent category, the range some experts on the subject deem acceptable.[17] Other kinds of property, like commercial buildings and lots, harder to assess because of less frequent sale of similar pieces, usually showed a still wider range. It is interesting to note, however, that assessment disparities seem to be diminishing across the country as a whole. The 1967 *Census of Governments* reports that for its sample of nonfarm houses, the coefficient of dispersion of the ratios of assessment values to sale prices dropped from an average 29.9 percent in 1956 to 25.8 percent in 1961 and 19.2 percent in 1966.[18]

Granted that improved assessment would not be likely to eliminate this dispersion entirely, the financial gains to city budgeters would be large if the lower half of the cases had their assessments raised to the former median. If we assume that 50 percent of the cases averaged 30 percent below the median at the outset, raising these to the median would increase the tax roll values by 15 percent, not to mention the reassessment gains that might accrue from raising some of those above the median. It seems quite unlikely that there would be much offsetting loss from reduced assessment when the usual ground for complaint is markedly diminished: "This other property is assessed lower than mine." The possibilities of exploiting that argument should be decreased, not increased. Both revenue and equity gains are possible.

In periods of relatively rapid price inflation, tax rolls lag seriously behind in most cities. Rising reproduction costs of both homes and commercial structures raise their sale values, and land values rise, too. The remedy is frequent general reassessments, but those are expensive, and too often city councils are reluctant to spend the money required even though the payoff would be large. The same is true in those cities where rapid population growth sends land values soaring. Most properties remain with values unchanged in the tax assessor's office because he and his staff have time to raise only the assessments of those properties that change hands. Even then, discovery of the sale price is not always easy because of anachronistic state laws that do not require full disclosure and the affixing of appropriate revenue stamps to the new deeds at the time they are recorded. City statutes might overcome this difficulty.

As suggested earlier, the adoption of statewide property classes would help reduce some of the resistance to attempts to equalize assessment ratios. Only 24 states now have such laws, although they are permitted under 31 state constitutions, and 15 out of the 24 have only partial systems. Existing medians could provide appropriate norms for the ratios assigned to each group[19] and thus remove much of the fear of substantial increases from reassessment. The movement toward greater equity would prove to be a move also toward greater revenue if, as seems likely from the frequency of downward reassessments on "grievance days," there are more low assessments to be raised than high assessments to be reduced.

Reforming the property tax along these lines has some economic and political disadvantages that should be noted. A rise in tax roll totals would not raise city revenues if it led to a loud clamor for a reduced property tax rate. Further, it might prove some additional stimulus to emigration, as previously explained. There is also the fact that some cities have purposely underassessed certain classes of property for various policy reasons, such as to attract new industry or to favor certain powerful economic interests.

Regardless of demonstrable revenue possibilities, there are political costs that may prove to be so great as to overcome the economic benefits. Consider, for instance, the outcry that would arise if each state were to take over the task of assessing all property and the many thousands of local assessors and staff, often political appointees, were to lose their jobs. There are approximately 18,000 primary assessment jurisdictions in the United States, many of them dealing with local areas so small that the average population per assessment district is only about 10,000. Furthermore, in any given year the number seeking reduced assessments under established grievance procedures is not large and would be far outnumbered by the host of property owners facing higher taxes if a general reassessment were to be carried out.

For similar political and economic reasons cities are unlikely to move strongly against another tempting target, tax exempt property. This belongs chiefly to nonprofit institutions like churches, schools, colleges, and hospitals. If these were to be put on the tax rolls, those which are presently receiving public subsidies would have to be given additional compensatory help, with no net gain. Others might close at social, if not economic, loss to the community. In most large cities there are also tax exempt state and federal office buildings. The total value of these tax exempt properties is considerable, having been estimated at 18 percent of the total assessed value of property in all cities—large and small. This is an average; in some cities it is much greater, as in Albany, N.Y. (46 percent), and Washington, D.C. (40 percent).[20] In addition, there is the partial exemption of veterans, of old people, and of poor people, as in the "circuit-breaker" arrangement just described. Some cities have a further exemption of some magnitude, that extended to new firms as an inducement to locate, but this occurs chiefly in smaller cities, not the large central cities from which the businesses are fleeing.

These exemptions have been mentioned to call attention to their frequently overlooked magnitude and hence their statistical potential for tax revenue. Political feasibility is something else again. Any exemptions that arise because of state or federal law can be changed only at those levels. By its own efforts a city can do little except to join with other cities in lobbying at state capitals or in Washington. Only exemptions created by the city itself can be repealed at home. Location incentives are a matter of contract. Special group exemptions arise because of political appeal, which becomes even stronger once hallowed by custom.

IS PROPERTY TAX RELIEF IN SIGHT?

Instead of seeking ways to increase property taxes, some seek to reduce them by obtaining additional tax revenues in other ways (which will be described below). Changes of this type may conceivably be forced on cities by court action as seemed likely in the early 1970's following some court decisions on the matter of school financing. For instance, the Federal District Court of Texas, Western Division, held in the Rodriguez case that "the current . . . system of financing public education in Texas discriminates on the basis of wealth by permitting citizens of affluent districts to provide a higher quality education for their children, while paying

lower taxes . . ." and accordingly "some new form of financing had
to be utilized to support public education with the restriction that
the program adopted not make the quality of public education as a
function of wealth other than the wealth of the state as a whole."
On direct appeal, however, the U.S. Supreme Court reversed the
District Court's decision.[21] As of the time of writing, American
public schools continue to be dependent upon property tax
revenues. In a parallel case (Serrano), the California Supreme Court
ruled that school spending that varies with local wealth violates the
California Constitution.[22] The legislature has, therefore, written a
new law to give $82 million of state money during 1973-74 to
school districts with substantial numbers of poor children. The law
also distributes additional state funds to reduce the property tax
rates in such districts.

Opposed as voters seem to be to property tax increases, they may
be even more opposed to replacing that tax as the mainstay of local
revenues. For example, in November 1972 voters in California,
Michigan, Colorado, and Oregon defeated proposals to abolish or
restrict the use of property taxes as a major source of funds for
schools. These proposals were put on the ballot by persons who
wanted the early Rodriguez court decision implemented as soon as
possible in the interests of better schools for the poor. Logical or
not from an economist's point of view, voters looked at the income
and sales tax alternatives and decided that in the matter of school
finance they would stay with the property tax.

In December 1972, the prestigious Advisory Commission on
Intergovernmental Relations, composed of members of the
President's Cabinet, governors, members of Congress and state
legislatures, mayors, and county officials, somewhat paradoxically
rejected President Nixon's idea that the federal government should
provide further financial aid to permit local governments to reduce
property taxes. The Commission is said to feel that homeowners
are in general overburdened by the residential property tax, yet the
Commission would not approve any additional federal assistance
(beyond the Federal Revenue Sharing Act of 1972) that would
permit a reduction in the property tax or make it fairer. The

Commission also voted specifically against a federal value-added tax as a substitute for part of the local property tax. As the *New York Times*'s correspondent reported, "It was not the idea of federal financial aid so much as aid tailored to a specific purpose that the group appeared to be voting against."[23]

SALES TAX POTENTIAL FOR CITIES

States have long used the retail sales tax, at first to raise additional revenue without having to raise property taxes and later to substitute for property taxes entirely. The withdrawal of state tax pressure on property is one reason why cities have been able to raise their property tax rates as high as they have. But now cities are adopting sales taxes, too, in their persistent quest for added revenue. Table 5.4 shows the increasing use of sales taxes as a percentage of total city revenue.

The main problem with sales taxation, whether general retail or special excise, as an urban revenue source is the same as with property taxation: the tendency to drive business away from the high tax rate localities. Escaping this tax is even easier than escaping a high property tax. Traveling to the suburbs to shop for major clothing and appliance items is not nearly so difficult as moving one's home or business. Whether the 1 or 2 percent saved is worthwhile or not depends upon the individual, the amount spent on taxable items, and the distance traveled. But the practice, once started, tends to become a habit, and only smaller, routine purchases are thereafter made for convenience in high-tax-area stores nearby. It is like the high-priced corner grocer losing business to the cheaper supermarket a mile or two away.

One very careful study of the New York City retail sales tax, for instance, shows the deleterious effects of the revenue gain. Stores in the central city suffered after it was imposed in 1934, and those in the suburbs prospered. As a result the demand for retail employees fell, and the unemployment rate among unskilled labor rose noticeably.[24] One might even argue from this experience that a further boost in the property tax might have been less detrimental. Of course, the two taxes do not fall entirely on the same people.

TABLE 5.4

City Sales and Gross Receipts Tax Revenues As a Percentage of General Revenue and of Own Resources

Year	General Sales and Gross Receipts Tax Revenues (in millions)	Percentage of General Revenue	Percentage of Own Resources
1955	$ 433	5.53%	6.78%
1960	797	6.84	8.54
1965	1,184	7.45	9.58
1970	1,948	7.31	10.40
1971	2,107	7.00	10.10

NOTE: In 1966 New York City replaced a gross receipts tax on business by a net income tax, resulting in a more than $200 million decline in reported general sales and gross receipts tax revenues between 1965–66 and 1966–67. The magnitude of New York City revenue figures affects the aggregate picture of all cities. In order to make the data for the years 1970 and 1971 comparable with the earlier period, the revenue of New York City from income taxes has been included in figures on general sales tax and gross receipts tax revenue, which would have been the case if the replacement of gross receipts tax on business by net income tax had not occurred.

SOURCE: U.S. Bureau of the Census, *City Government Finances*, for various years.

And the question of who should bear the burden, is a value judgment that clearly is influenced by personal interest and class feeling.

THE PERSONAL INCOME TAX FOR CITIES

Some cities have turned to the personal income tax to avoid having to raise property and sales taxes or, in many cases, apparently to avoid using the sales tax at all. Revenues raised in this manner are still very small but are rising rapidly, as shown in Table. 5.5. This tax is harder to evade than the others. If city dwellers move to the suburbs or shop in the suburbs they may evade the property tax or sales tax. But if they continue to work within the central city, they can be forced to pay its income tax levy through laws requiring collection at the source. Although the rate is occasionally lower for commuters than for residents, only by getting a new job in the suburbs can they escape the tax entirely.

TABLE 5.5

Urban Revenues from Personal Income Tax, 1960 and 1972
(48 largest cities)

Year	Total Income Tax Revenue (in millions)	Percentage of Total General Revenues	Percentage of Revenues from Own Resources
1960	$ 174	2.54%	3.63%
1972	1,575	8.17	13.36

SOURCE: U.S. Bureau of the Census, *City Government Finances,* 1960 and 1971–72.

USER CHARGES AND OTHER WAYS FOR CITIES
TO RAISE ADDITIONAL REVENUE

There is yet another way for hard-pressed cities to raise additional revenue. They may impose new service charges or raise old ones. These charges include billing for such things as sewers, refuse pick-up, licenses, water (if municipally owned), hospital use, and some higher education and adult education. Many cities have not raised these fees and prices enough to compensate for recent inflationary increases in the costs of providing the services. Other fees were established initially on an arbitrary basis without good cost accounting. It seems likely that inflation adjustments alone would raise total revenue substantially in this category. Some charges could be raised above cost to provide revenue for the general budget of cities as has been done with electric rates in some smaller municipalities that have public ownership of power plants.

In this area, as in all other sources of revenue, there are considerations other than just the possibility of getting more money. Some services have been underpriced intentionally to stimulate use, as with adult and higher education, or to subsidize the poor, as with hospital care. Whether these rates should be raised or not, or how much they should be raised, is as much a matter of social policy as of fiscal pressure. Demand, however, is probably quite inelastic, except perhaps for education, and higher user charges would produce more total revenue in both the short run and the long run. Table 5.6 shows the trend for all user charges for all cities for the period 1955-71.

TABLE 5.6

Trend of City Revenues from User Charges

Year	Revenue from User Charges (in millions)	Percentage of Total General Revenues	Percentage of Revenues from Own Resources
1955	$ 756	9.66%	11.84%
1960	1,342	11.52	14.39
1965	1,951	12.28	15.80
1970	3,113	11.70	16.63
1971	3,579	11.70	17.14

SOURCE: U.S. Bureau of the Census, *City Government Finances*, for various years.

Second Alternative:
Intergovernmental Aid As a Rational Choice

Some see state and federal aid as the last resort for our unfortunate cities, the only way to bail them out of their fiscal difficulties. While that may be true for some of them, the poorest and the most heavily taxed, it is definitely not true for all of them and probably not true for most. One must beware of looking at New York City and generalizing about cities from that exceptional case—or at Newark or Detroit, to mention two middle-sized cities that are in definite financial difficulties.

A variety of arguments supports the call for increased inter-governmental aid. Some public services performed by local governments benefit an area far larger than the taxing district. Take education, for instance. With a population as mobile as that of the United States, the chance of a boy educated in the public schools of a given city remaining there the rest of his life is less than 50-50, a truth long recited by sociologists and recently popularized by Vance Packard in his book *A Nation of Strangers.* If the benefit is state-wide or nationwide, why not charge the costs to all the taxpayers of the state or to all those of the nation rather than just to those of the particular city?

The argument for wider financing through intergovernmental aid becomes even more compelling when we recall the continuing migration from the countryside to the cities. To the extent that these migrants are poor, as a large proportion of them are, they place additional burdens on the cities while relieving the burdens of the places from which they come. It seems reasonable to predict that this trend will continue and accelerate. If the cities are seen as places of refuge for the nation's poor, it is logical that the nation as a whole should bear part of the cities' cost of making life tolerable for the poor by various forms of welfare assistance, training for jobs, and so forth.

Education and welfare are not the only functions of this type. Health is another. Public health services and hospitals partly supported by tax monies frequently serve a larger area than is taxed to finance them. Commuters daily use city streets and depend on city police and fire protection as they come in from the suburbs to their central city jobs. Other outsiders, even out-of-staters, travel those streets in visiting or passing through the city. City parks and recreational facilities are not restricted to the use of city dwellers.

Still another line of reasoning supports the trend toward increasing intergovernmental aid to cities. It is based on the idea that people as citizens have the right to equality in governmental services wherever they may live and that the cost of providing those services should be distributed on the basis of ability to pay. If the older and larger cities have more than their share of the poor, as they do, they also usually lack the per capita revenue base of younger and smaller cities. At the same time, they need to spend more per capita to care for the greater needs of the poor. Equalization of services can come partly from greater than average fiscal effort. Table 5.7 shows that this has happened. All those with more "poor" (Social Security Administration definition) than the national average of 11 percent show a fiscal effort above the 4.3 percent national average for all cities. Comparing the ratios suggests kudos especially for Washington, Boston, Newark, and New York. But their effort is not enough. The heavily taxed cities need still more money and frequently feel they can get it only from governments above—that is, through grants financed by the tax sources open to states or the federal government.

TABLE 5.7

Poverty-Saddled Cities Make Unusual Fiscal Effort in 1970

City	Percentage of Population Classed As Poor	Fiscal Effort in 1970 (Revenue Per Capita from Own Resources/Per Capita Income)
Newark	18.4%	12.1
Norfolk	16.1	7.4
St. Louis	14.3	8.1
Baltimore	14.0	9.7
Cleveland	13.4	6.0
Louisville	13.0	6.7
Cincinnati	12.8	9.7
Washington, D.C.	12.7	15.5
Boston	11.7	13.9
New York	11.5	12.0
Detroit	11.3	6.0
Philadelphia	11.2	7.8
All cities	11.0	4.3

SOURCES: U.S. Bureau of the Census, *City Government Finances, 1969–70;* and *idem, General Social and Economic Characteristics, U.S. Summary,* 1972.

A final rational argument for intergovernmental aid to cities deals with the allocation of resources in our economy. It goes back to what was said several times earlier: that high taxes in the large cities tend to drive people away from the disadvantaged city to surrounding communities with lower taxes. They take their tax-paying abilities with them. To the extent that this occurs it causes a reallocation of the nation's resources, based not on market forces, but on the political accidents of differential tax burdens. It may increase the travel time of workers, extend the shipping distances for raw materials and finished products, and cause untimely replacement of old but still serviceable buildings by new ones. All of this is uneconomical. Hence the logic of intergovernmental aid, which can reduce even if it cannot eliminate the tax burden differential now so unfavorable to many of our large cities.

INTERGOVERNMENTAL AID:
IN EXISTENCE AND GROWING

Cities would be in much worse fiscal trouble than they are today if it were not for the intergovernmental aid their taxpayers have been receiving for some time. Table 5.8 shows that city governments have received from 15 to 30 percent of their total revenues from state and federal grants for thirty years. State aid is nothing new.

The major part of state aid to local governments has been for education. It amounted to 60 percent of the total in 1969, compared with 18 percent for public welfare and 8.5 percent for highways. Federal aid to local governments went 25 percent for welfare ("income security"), 15 percent for education, 15 percent for health, and 8 percent for community development and housing.[25]

More significant for our purposes than these figures is the trend in combined federal and state aid. Total intergovernmental aid to local governments rose more rapidly in the sixties than in the fifties, about 160 percent compared with 130 percent. At the same time, total local spending was rising less rapidly, so that inter-governmental aid as a percentage of total revenue rose from 20 in

TABLE 5.8

State and Federal Aid to Cities
(In millions)

Fiscal Year	Revenue from Own Sources	State and Federal Aid	Total General Revenues	State-Federal Aid As Percentage of Total Revenues
1942	$ 2,620	$ 491	$ 3,111	15.7%
1952	5,139	1,212	6,351	19.1
1955	6,386	1,438	7,824	18.3
1960	9,326	2,321	11,647	19.9
1965	12,350	3,534	15,884	22.2
1970	18,715	7,906	26,621	29.6
1971	20,878	9,697	30,575	31.7
1972	23,502	11,434	34,937	32.7

SOURCES: U.S. Bureau of the Census, *Statistical Abstract of the United States*, 1972, p. 426; idem, *Historical Statistics on Governmental Finances and Employment*, 1967, p. 48; idem, *City Government Finances*, 1971–72; and Tax Foundation, *Facts and Figures on Government Finance* (New York, 1971), p. 241.

1960 to 33 percent in 1972. It is this sort of uptrend that must continue if cities are to experience less fiscal distress in the future.

CATEGORICAL INTERGOVERNMENTAL AID

The traditional form of intergovernmental aid is that extended for a particular purpose (i.e., in a specific category) such as education, welfare, or housing. One-third of federal aid to state and local governments recently has been for "income security," more popularly known as "public welfare." Three other categories each received from 15 percent to 20 percent of the federal grant-in-aid total: education and manpower training, health, and community development and housing. The last group and welfare showed the most rapid recent growth. Nearly all of this money was funneled down to local governments, chiefly for the benefit of city dwellers.

State grants to local governments for education in 1969 included $4 billion received from the federal government and nearly $11 billion from state revenue sources, a total of about $15 billion. For welfare in various forms, total state contributions were $4.4 billion, practically all of which came from Washington. Local governments added another $1.2 billion of their own funds, making their total direct expenditure for public welfare needs in that year approximately $5.6 billion. Table 5.9 shows the amounts of state payments to local governments by functions for several representative fiscal years.[26] The relative rates of increase of the major categories of intergovernmental aid may be read from Figure 5.2 (the more rapid the growth, the steeper the line segment).

TABLE 5.9

State Payments to Local Governments by Functions, Selected Years, 1922–71

(In millions)

Fiscal Year	Total	Education	Highways	Welfare	Other Specified	Other Unspecified
1922	$ 312	$ 202	—	—	—	—
1932	801	398	$ 229	—	—	$ 140
1940	1,654	700	332	$ 420	—	180
1950	4,217	2,054	610	792	$ 279	482
1957	7,439	4,212	1,083	1,136	340	668
1960	9,443	5,461	1,247	1,483	446	806
1965	14,174	8,351	1,630	2,436	654	1,102
1969	24,779	14,858	2,109	4,402	1,275	2,135
1970	28,892	17,085	2,439	5,003	1,407	2,958
1971	32,640	19,292	2,507	5,760	1,823	3,258

SOURCES: U.S. Bureau of the Census, *State Government Finances*, for various years; and Tax Foundation, *Facts and Figures on Government Finance* (New York, 1971).

As explained earlier, city governments are narrower in scope than the group known as "local governments," which include

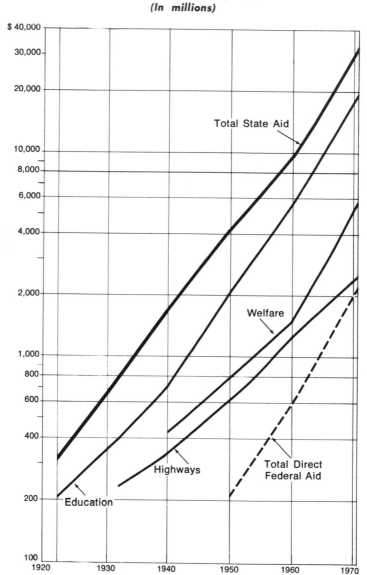

FIGURE 5.2

Rise in Aid to Local Governments from States and Directly
from Federal Government, 1922–71
(In millions)

unconsolidated school districts, counties, and other overlapping political entities. Therefore, when we find that in 1972 cities received only $11.4 billion in total intergovernmental aid, both federal and state, while "local governments" obtained a total about three and a half times as large, $39.0 billion, we should not be surprised. Most important to cities is how adequately this aid from above helps them meet the expenditures that remain in their budgets after the costs of functions like schools and welfare are largely or entirely assumed by other governmental units.

Categorical aid reaching cities directly and indirectly has been of great assistance to them. In 1969 it helped them meet expenses by adding to their spending capacity an amount equal to about 50 percent of the revenues they raised internally by taxes and charges. At the same time it seems to have stimulated city spending by about one-third, according to a study of the 1967 budgets of the 43 largest U.S. cities.[27]

Categorical aid is a mixed blessing, however. It enables cities to provide additional services, but the matching funds requirement forces cities to raise more taxes.[28] As a result, taxpayer protest sometimes outweighs recipient clamor. Furthermore, some cities have priorities in areas other than those for which specific aid is offered. This is one reason for wanting to substitute general revenue sharing.

MEASURING FISCAL CAPACITY

If we knew the capacity of a distressed city to raise revenue to pay its expenses, we would have some basis for deciding whether its alleged fiscal difficulties stemmed from unusual need, from substandard effort, or from below average ability to pay. Grant programs could then be adjusted accordingly, rewarding those with inferior capacity and unusual need but withholding funds from those unwilling to make at least average fiscal effort.

How, then, should fiscal capacity be measured? Some states have used property values in their aid formulas, making grants to cities in inverse proportion to the assessed value per capita of property on the tax rolls. This approach stems from the general

TABLE 5.10

Assessed and Adjusted Market Value Per Capita of Ordinary Real Estate in 41 Cities, 1967
(In ascending order of per capita adjusted market value)

City	Assessed Value	Adjusted Market Value	City	Assessed Value	Adjusted Market Value
Jacksonville	$ 930	$1,093	Nashville	$1,210	$ 3,830
Indianapolis	636	1,995	Cleveland	1,427	3,836
Memphis	973	2,152	Cincinnati	1,687	3,859
Baltimore	1,723	2,523	New Orleans	868	4,042
New York	1,319	2,681	St. Paul	381	4,135
Buffalo	1,918	2,775	Toledo	1,544	4,164
Philadelphia	1,644	2,830	Denver	1,241	4,340
Norfolk	1,140	3,026	Miami	3,128	4,376
Boston	1,172	3,100	San Jose	962	4,543
St. Louis	1,297	3,164	San Diego	958	4,722
Atlanta	769	3,191	Minneapolis	495	4,864
Pittsburgh	1,421	3,258	Washington, D.C.	2,122	4,968
Chicago	1,372	3,356	Oklahoma City	820	4,975
Omaha	1,086	3,398	Portland	1,026	4,982
Detroit	1,412	3,453	Seattle	906	5,524
Tulsa	819	3,527	Long Beach	1,061	5,582
Kansas City	932	3,535	Los Angeles	1,222	6,236
Birmingham	930	3,551	Oakland	969	6,503
Phoenix	703	3,742	San Francisco	774	7,038
Columbus	1,444	3,781	Honolulu	6,089	10,046
Milwaukee	1,946	·3,808			

NOTE: For computing per capita values, 1970 population figures have been used.

SOURCE: U.S. Bureau of the Census, *Census of Governments, 1967*, Vol. 2, *Taxable Property Values* (Washington, D.C., 1968), pp. 148 and 149.

reliance on property taxation to finance public schools and other local expenditures. The richer a community by this measure, the more it should be expected to finance its own needs and the less to rely upon the state government. Table 5.10 shows how much poorer some cities are than others when ranked according to this criterion. It is interesting to note the changes in rank that occur when adjusted market values are substituted for local tax roll assessment figures, but statistical errors (sampling, computations, etc.) must be assumed to account for some of the rankings.

Another measure of ability to pay is income per capita, per worker, or per family. Estimates of city income per capita have been made by the Bureau of the Census and also by *Sales Management,* a monthly magazine. The ones with the lowest incomes we could call the poorest, but we have no absolute figures to serve as a poverty cut-off line. Another approach to the definition of poverty is to call "poor" the lowest quarter of the 48 largest cities for which detailed data are available. Table 5.11 applies this criterion to two different estimates. One is per capita income as defined by the Bureau of the Census and the other is "effective per capita buying power" calculated by a complex formula devised by *Sales Management.* The latter estimates are higher than the former because *Sales Management* includes transfer payments, imputed rents of owner occupied homes, and other items; the magazine says that "more than 300 separate calculations" are required to determine the effective buying power totals.

The lists are not identical because of differences in the way income was estimated. The reason for presenting this table is not to single out certain cities by name but rather to show that substantial income differences do exist and that a grant formula could be devised that would distribute assistance according to fiscal weakness. The table also shows that the base chosen for the allocations would affect substantially the amounts received by individual cities.

Relative tax-paying capacity may also be derived directly from tax collections themselves. Cities make use of many types of taxes—property, income, sales, etc.—but in different pro-

TABLE 5.11

"Poor" Large Cities of the United States, by Two Measures

Census Bureau Estimates, 12 Cities, 1970		Sales Management Estimates, 12 Cities, 1971	
City	Per Capita Income	City	Effective Buying Power, Per Capita Income
El Paso	$2,409	San Antonio	$2,735
Newark	2,498	El Paso	2,854
Birmingham	2,577	Norfolk	2,928
San Antonio	2,581	Miami	3,085
New Orleans	2,723	Baltimore	3,117
St. Louis	2,737	Nashville	3,151
Norfolk	2,797	Memphis	3,184
Memphis	2,797	St. Louis	3,190
Miami	2,844	Cleveland	3,284
Jacksonville	2,871	Jacksonville	3,303
Cleveland	2,849	Fort Worth	3,412
Baltimore	2,886	Columbus	3,429

NOTE: A "poor" city is defined as one that is in the lowest quarter of the 48 largest cities.

SOURCES: U.S. Bureau of the Census, Census of Population: General Social and Economic Characteristics, 1970; and Editors of Sales Management, "1972 Survey of Buying Power," Sales Management, July 10, 1972.

portions in different cities. They also employ a variety of user charges. The Advisory Commission for Intergovernmental Relations argues that a good estimate of relative revenue capacity may be obtained by lumping all tax incomes and sources together. No arbitrary uniform weighting of each for all cities seems as appropriate as a national average. The formal definition of revenue capacity proposed by the ACIR is, therefore, "the total amount of revenue that would result by applying, within the area, the national average rate of each of the numerous kinds of . . . local revenue sources."[29] Fiscal effort then becomes "the percentage relation between the actual amounts of revenue obtained by governments . . . and their revenue capacity, as estimated by the 'average-financing-system' approach." This means that for the nation as a whole, actual revenue equals total revenue capacity and each city's fiscal effort figure shows how its performance compared with the national average in that year.

One major advantage of this approach over the per capita income or property value measures is that it properly allows for overlapping jurisdictions of taxing and financing districts. For instance, cities that are fiscally distinct from the school districts serving their inhabitants are treated on the same basis as those that have consolidated their school financing into city budgets. The same is true for county-supported health and welfare functions. Adjustments were also made for interstate differences. This is a "real world" formula, not someone's ideal pattern of taxation. It weighs property taxation higher than most economists would prefer and income taxes much lower; but that is how things were done in fiscal 1966-67 and represents a national pattern that changes only slowly.

A disadvantage is that data were not available for the ACIR to make appropriate calculations for nearly half of the 130 cities of more than 100,000 population (1960 Census). The curtailed list of 69 cities, however, shows a wide variation in revenue-raising capacity, which is our main point. They range from Long Beach at 186 percent of the national average down to Scranton at 82 percent, more than 2 to 1. Eleven of the top 15 are from the West Coast. Of the bottom 15, 8 cluster about Pennsylvania, but the rest are scattered. (See Table 5.12.)

FISCAL EFFORT AS A POLICY GUIDE
IN MAKING GRANTS

If one is seeking an appropriate measure of city differences for use in an equalizing grant program, it could make a big difference to recipient cities which of the three capacity formulas was used. A fourth approach would be to employ a measure of revenue effort as a substitute for revenue capacity or as a supplement to it. Revenue

TABLE 5.12

**ACIR Measure of Per Capita Revenue Capacity for 30 Cities
of Over 100,000 Population, 1966–67**

Highest Revenue Capacity		Lowest Revenue Capacity	
Long Beach	$372	Honolulu	$201
Chattanooga	368	Baltimore	201
Pasadena	346	Youngstown	200
Seattle	332	Philadelphia	199
Winston-Salem	326	Columbus (Ohio)	198
Sacramento	312	Spokane	198
Los Angeles	309	Allentown	197
New York	305	Albuquerque	189
Glendale	305	Birmingham	179
Kansas City	304	Baton Rouge	179
Anaheim	304	Canton	179
Portland	301	Erie	168
Oakland	299	Mobile	167
Tacoma	299	Tucson	166
Torrance	296	Scranton	164

NOTE: These are the top 15 and the bottom 15 in a list of 69; the average capacity was $200, the median $235.

SOURCES: ACIR, *Measuring the Fiscal Capacity and Effort of State and Local Areas* (Washington, D.C., 1971), p. 89; and idem, *Information Report Revision,* March 1972.

effort may be defined as the ratio between per capita revenue raised and per capita capacity. The poorer a city the more effort needed to raise a given revenue amount per capita. A formula could be devised that rewarded above-average effort in addition to compensating for below-average capacity. Including effort in the formula is in keeping with the Puritan ethic and might stimulate cities to try harder to raise money at home in their efforts either to cope with abnormal needs or to provide superior services, like police protection or educational facilities.

To illustrate what it might mean to apply a "fiscal effort" criterion to American cities, Table 5.13 has been prepared to show

TABLE 5.13

Large Cities with a Revenue Effort More Than 10 Percent Above Average, 1966–67

City	Relative Revenue Effort	Relative Revenue Capacity
Boston	139	85
Tucson	133	83
Cincinnati	133	127
New York	131	149
Anaheim	131	140
Berkeley	131	121
San Jose	126	117
St. Petersburg	124	113
Baltimore	118	99
Los Angeles	117	153
Oakland	117	149
Dayton	117	116
Philadelphia	115	95
San Diego	112	113
Topeka	111	90
Akron	111	108
Some Others		
Chicago	97	124
St. Louis	108	131
Denver	107	136
Washington, D.C.	70	117
New Orleans	75	111
Cleveland	103	121
Seattle	84	159

NOTE: The figures for relative revenue effort and capacity are per capita ones based on a U.S. average of 100.

SOURCE: ACIR, *Measuring the Fiscal Capacity and Effort of State and Local Areas* (Washington, D.C., 1971), p. 89.

those 16 cities in the ACIR list of 69 cities that made the greatest effort in 1966-67.[30] It is interesting to note that five of these cities, including the two at the top of the list in effort, had below average revenue capacities, while the rest had above average capacity, as did the other large cities added for comparison. It appears that there is little correlation between capacity and effort.

THE STATE AND LOCAL FISCAL ASSISTANCE ACT OF 1972

In 1972 the federal government for the first time appropriated money for aid to state and local governments without specifying the activity it should help finance. This is a radical departure from the categorical aid patterns of the past and was designed to supplement them, not supplant them. It started at $5.3 billion a year for 1972, rising gradually to approximately $6.5 billion in 1976, or an average of about $6 billion a year for the five years. The aid was divided roughly one-third to states and two-thirds to local governments.

The distribution formula determines how much each city gets by first making a division among the states, then among the counties, and finally among the cities and other local governments within the counties, except school districts and other special-purpose governmental units. A federal publication summarizes the process as follows:

> General Revenue Sharing funds are distributed among States on the basis of one of two formulas. The "three factor" formula distributes the funds on the basis of population, tax effort, and per capita income. The "five factor" formula includes two additional factors, urbanized population and the State income tax collections. Each state amount is determined by the formula that maximizes its share. If the total of the shares is greater than the available authorization, all shares are reduced proportionally.
>
> Within the State one-third of all funds go to the State government, two-thirds to local governments. Distribution

among local governments is based on the three-factor formula.[31]

From the foregoing one may infer that how much any given city gets from the General Revenue Sharing program is a function, first, of the state in which it is located; second, of its county; and third, of how it compares with other local governments in that county in per capita tax capacity and tax effort. The poorer states get more and so do those that are making a strong tax effort (effort being defined as "net tax collections divided by aggregate personal income"). The same determinants operate the rest of the way down, from state to county to city. Therefore we cannot make direct comparisons between cities across the nation; rather, we have to consider each city's allotment as the end of a chain formula. When we find New York City at the top of the list in per capita revenue-sharing allotments for the first year (see Table 5.14), we explain this, first, by saying that New York State ranks high because of substantial tax effort and extensive urbanization factors which offset its high rank in the revenue scale; and second, by noting that the city itself scores high because of its high tax effort within the state. In contrast, Boston's high rank is related more to its own high tax effort in the face of low tax capacity than to its location in a high-grant state (Massachusetts ranks 20th from the top in state allocations).

Turning to cities at the bottom of the list in Table 5.14, we find Atlanta, San Diego, and Houston, whose states receive moderate allotments under the program. Atlanta shows a low tax effort and a relatively high median income, both of which militate against its getting much under the General Revenue Sharing formula. Somewhat the same situation prevails for the other two cities, according to available data. Lacking the precise figures used by the Treasury in calculating the revenue-sharing grants, we cannot explain the exact position of every city in Table 5.14, but the general intention of the program is clear: to compensate for relative poverty and to reward relative effort. (Of course, superior effort may itself be a result of unusual poverty-related service demands.) The new pro-

TABLE 5.14

Per Capita Allocations for 28 Large Cities Under Federal General Revenue Sharing, 1972

New York	$31.3
Boston	27.7
San Francisco	26.9
Baltimore	26.4
New Orleans	24.7
Detroit	24.1
Denver	23.7
Pittsburgh	22.5
Philadelphia	22.5
Chicago	20.6
St. Louis	20.4
Kansas	18.9
Cleveland	18.8
Cincinnati	18.7
Seattle	18.6
Phoenix	15.9
Memphis	15.7
Buffalo	15.7
Milwaukee	15.6
Columbus	15.5
Nashville	15.0
Los Angeles	12.6
San Antonio	11.9
Dallas	11.4
Houston	11.4
Minneapolis	11.0
San Diego	9.3
Atlanta	9.2

SOURCE: Calculated from ACIR, *Information Bulletin 72–8*, October 9, 1972.

gram was devised to satisfy both a sense of justice and the Protestant ethic. Moreover, no general-purpose local government is left out entirely: there is something for everyone. This feature undoubtedly contributed to the huge success of the bill in Congress.

Actually, the per capita dollar allotment that a city receives from the Federal government is not as important as how much it amounts to as a percentage of total city spending (see Table 5.15). By this criterion federal revenue sharing was not very important in the city budgets of New York, Boston, San Francisco, and Baltimore, even though these four were at the top of the per capita list. On the other hand, New Orleans, Denver, and Pittsburgh are found near the top of both lists, and there is no general shifting of relative city positions from one list to the next.

Interestingly, states are permitted to pass laws changing the formulas for allocating funds among county areas or local governments, including cities. They may omit either of the two variables, per capita tax effort or per capita income—i.e., level of spending or ability to pay. The former reflects community needs or desires, the latter its difficulty in meeting those needs.

The ACIR summarized its view of the probable impact of federal general revenue sharing as follows:

Any new source of money—particularly with no strings—is very welcome to states, counties, and cities contemplating tax increases and budget cuts. Revenue sharing will account for about one to two percent of state budgets, generally five to ten percent of city budgets. . . .

Revenue sharing is no panacea. It will not rescue the cities from total bankruptcy. But it will buy time—as much as two or three years—for cities to balance their budgets without needing a large tax hike . . . expenditures will eat up revenue sharing allocations in a few years. Of twenty-eight major cities, twelve will receive less from revenue sharing than the expenditure increase in their general funds for the most recent one-year period.[32]

TABLE 5.15

Revenue-Sharing Allocations Compared with City General Fund Operating Expenditures
(In millions)

City	General Fund Expenditures	One-Year Increase in Expenditures [a]	Revenue-Sharing Allocation	Revenue Sharing As a Percentage of Expenditures
New Orleans	$ 67.7	$ 7.1	$ 14.7	21.7%
Chicago	382.0	52.1	69.5	18.2
Kansas City	61.0	6.3	10.2	16.7
Seattle	62.3	9.0	9.9	15.9
San Antonio	49.2	3.3	7.8	15.8
Nashville	41.5	3.0	6.4	15.4
Cincinnati	56.4	5.5	8.5	15.1
Cleveland	95.0	−10.8	14.1	14.8
Denver	83.6	8.7	12.2	14.6
Pittsburgh	87.0	1.3	11.7	13.4
Phoenix	69.8	11.6	9.3	13.3
Memphis	79.7	8.1	9.8	12.3
Los Angeles	294.0	31.5	35.4	12.0
Minneapolis	40.8	3.6	4.8	11.8
Columbus (Ohio)	49.9	7.5	5.7	11.4
Dallas	90.1	5.6	9.7	10.8
Houston	129.7	16.8	14.0	10.8
San Diego	63.6	5.6	6.5	10.2
St. Louis	124.9	15.2	12.7	10.2
Buffalo	79.7	6.5	7.3	9.2
Milwaukee	130.3	17.7	11.2	8.6
Philadelphia	526.7	67.8	43.8	8.3
Detroit	440.7	55.8	36.5	8.3
Atlanta	60.5	7.9	4.6	7.6
Baltimore [b]	390.7	29.6	23.9	6.1
Boston [b]	315.6	55.2	17.8	5.6
San Francisco [b]	492.4	77.2	19.3	3.9 (5.4)[c]
New York [b]	7,772.0	912.4	247.5	3.2 (5.5)[c]

[a] The source states that the expenditure increase figures were taken from data for the most recent year available for each city.

[b] General fund expenditures for these cities include substantial amounts for education and welfare that were either handled as a separate fund or were not a major city responsibility for the other cities studied.

[c] Adjusted for expenditures on education and welfare.

SOURCE: ACIR, *Information Bulletin 72–8*, October 19, 1972. The source states that the figures for revenue-sharing allocations are based on the Joint Committee on Internal Revenue Taxation, *Supplemental Report Showing Distribution of Funds As Agreed to by Congress*, under the State and Local Fiscal Assistance Act of 1972.

GENERAL REVENUE SHARING: SOME COMMENTS

In addition to their need for more money, cities also want greater freedom in the use of grant funds. In the mid-sixties they began campaigning for some form of general revenue sharing and were successful in a few states. During 1969, $2.1 billion was distributed in this form by states to local governments, an amount less than 10 percent of the total of categorical grants. The ACIR was a strong advocate of this development also at the federal level "as a tool to help States and local governments stand on their own fiscal and political feet—to strengthen their fiscal responsibility and political self-reliance."[33] This line of argument was well calculated to appeal to fiscal conservatives in Washington and probably helped the 1972 general revenue sharing bill win presidential and congressional support. So also did the fact that the formula adopted provided something for everyone. However, the main reason for widespread support from state and local governments was undoubtedly financial: this was now a source for badly needed additional funds.

Economists, too, were likely to approve of increased federal aid to states and localities, but for different reasons. Their concern is with the limits to the nation's resources and the desirability of minimizing the adverse effects of taxation. This leads them in general to favor the relatively progressive federal tax system over clearly regressive state or local taxes because taxation based on ability to pay is thought to cause less human hurt. A minority among economists has always argued against progressive taxes, believing that they restrict output and growth and are thus economically harmful. That argument, however, applies to the whole of the federal income tax and not specifically to federal revenue sharing.

Despite all this support for revenue sharing, the federal government faces the same basic fiscal problems that confront states and cities. When its expenditures rise as theirs do, for whatever reason, funds must be found. That means raising taxes, finding new sources of revenue, cutting other expenses, or borrowing. Higher federal taxes on personal incomes or corporate profits tend to be viewed as unfavorably in Washington as higher property or sales taxes at home, and the other choices are also distasteful.

It is interesting to set the revenue-sharing proposal in historical perspective. There was a time in the early sixties when economists spoke about "fiscal drag," the apparent inability of the federal government to spend all of its "growth dividend." The tax base seemed to grow so rapidly that it yielded increased tax revenues faster than the money could be spent. This surplus tended to depress the economy, to slow its rate of growth. At the same time states and local governments, as we have seen, were suffering from the opposite plight: their revenues did not expand rapidly enough. This led Walter Heller and others to propose general revenue sharing as a way to solve both problems at the same time.[34]

The Vietnam War and Pentagon pressures for new weapons destroyed that happy solution. Federal tax cuts in 1964 and again in 1969-71 also contributed to the disappearance of the budget surpluses of the early sixties. The resurrection of the revenue-sharing proposal in the early seventies was intended only to bail out cities and states, strictly a one-sided proposition. By that time the talk in Washington was how the federal government could hold down total spending even though, for political reasons, it chose to expand aid to lower-level governments out of revenues that were no longer surplus. That meant cutting somewhere else to avoid raising federal taxes, or imposing a value-added tax with its clearly regressive features, or adding to the inflation problem by deficit spending, a situation which is itself a form of regressive taxation. Of course, military spending could be cut, but proposals in that area arouse the opposition of the country's most potent lobbies with their effective "national security" propaganda. The other major items in our federal budget are associated with income security, health, and interest payments on public debt. Paradoxically, the first two lie in the area of existing categorical grants to state and local governments. It is probable that some of these will be cut, as in the budget proposed for 1974, to avoid raising taxes. The cities may find Washington giving with one hand and taking back with the other.

One even hears that the lower-level governments are becoming affluent while the federal government is being asked to assume more of their costs, as the American Enterprise Institute said in 1972.[35] Cities don't see it that way and feel that their needs are genuine and persistent. They want general revenue sharing as a supplement to categorical grants, not as a a substitute for them. They intend to use its bounty to pay for services and facilities otherwise foregone, to gain spending flexibility, or to permit some reduction in existing tax rates.

Assuming the state and local governments emerge with a net gain, then how much the new general revenue-sharing policy solves their fiscal problems depends on several factors. One is the size of the net gain, which is related to the level of all kinds of revenue sharing, especially after 1976. Another is the rate of increase in local needs and wants. Third is the willingness and ability to pay local costs at home. Fourth is the formula used to disburse the revenue that the federal government is willing to share with lower-level governments.

URBAN SPECIAL REVENUE-SHARING PROPOSALS
FOR 1974 AND THEREAFTER

When the Nixon Administration decided to propose drastic cuts in federal categorical grants for social programs in fiscal 1974 and thereafter, state and local governments faced an annual reduction of more than $5.6 billion in federal aid commitments, about one-third of the amount provided in fiscal 1973. Much of this impact would ultimately be on cities, even though most of the money went first to state treasuries and then to local governments or to state agencies that administered programs which benefited urban residents. Four grant areas were consolidated into "Special Revenue Sharing": education, manpower training, law enforcement assistance, and urban community development.[36] This last included seven categorical grant programs, particularly the urban renewal and model cities programs. Existing programs are to be liquidated from 1975 through 1977. New funds under the administration's urban special revenue-sharing proposals begin to be available in 1975 at $560 million and rise to $2.3 billion in 1978. For 1974 there will be no new federal money for new projects in urban development, but money already committed ($1.9 billion) for the old categorical grants being terminated will be provided to cities according to existing contracts.

At the time of writing, congressional debate on the Better Communities Act of 1973, which provided for the changeover to block grants, was not completed, but the general push in that direction was unmistakeable. Most big city mayors seem to welcome the greater control over community development money that the block grant approach would deliver by 1977, even if the total is slightly less than that of the seven categorical grants being terminated as of 1974. Urban special revenue sharing seems destined to join general revenue sharing as the wave of the future. How big that wave will be and how much supplemented by the other categorical grant programs that remain is a political question, one of the power that can be wielded by city spokesmen in the national capital. The Nixon budget would favor cities over 1 million, urban counties, and state discretionary funds.

THE CANADIAN APPROACH: USING A REVENUE
   EQUALIZING FORMULA

In 1967 Canada passed a law to provide special aid from the federal government to those provinces that seemed to be in need because of below average tax capacity. This was estimated by first taking the total revenue raised for provincial use by 16 different taxes and dividing it by the total tax base for each. That gave 16 average tax rates for the nation, which then were applied to each individual province. The total potential revenue thus raised was considered an indication of the province's tax capacity. Where it was less than the national average on per capita basis, the province was granted enough to bring it up to par. The total cost to the United States if such a formula were applied here to needy states was estimated by the ACIR to be about 5 percent of own-source revenues, or $1.8 billion based on 1966-67 figures.[37]

The ACIR has made no separate estimate of the cost of revenue equalization grants to U.S. cities, but its calculation of the results of applying the formula to state and local revenue capacity versus state alone is indicative. Including all localities, the total cost is raised to $4.6 billion, an increase of $2.8 billion. The change is explained by citing the below average fiscal effort of localities in 19 of the 25 states that would have received federal grants under this formula. Twelve of these states were south of the Mason-Dixon line (but Florida and Louisiana scored above average).[38]

Differences between the Canadian 1967 and the U.S. 1972 grant formulae in this type of fiscal relationship are, first, the absence in Canada of an effort criterion and, second, the different ways of measuring capacity. Canada's approach to "fiscal capacity" resembles that of the ACIR, but it was not carried down to the local level. The Canadian provinces are free to use the revenue-equalizing grants for their own budgeting and do not have to pass part of them on to cities and other local governments. In that sense, they have fewer strings attached to their assistance program than we do.

Canadian equalization grants go only to the seven poorest provinces—there is nothing for the top three. This cuts down on the total cost to the federal government, something that should appeal to fiscal conservatives in Washington. It is analogous to a negative income tax with a cut-off point at some poverty line, as opposed to the something-for-everyone American plan.[39] Canada taxes all to aid a few; we tax all to aid all. Having once started a relatively expensive universal assistance program, we are unlikely, even in a quest for economy, to go back to a plan that helps only the poorer cities and states. However, it is interesting to note how a Canadian type of formula would work out in this country. The ACIR has calculated that it would have taken $5.8 billion in 1968-69 to bring up to the national average the per capita revenue capacity of all state and local governments that were below par, a figure approximately the same as the $6 billion average annual cost of the 1972 "something-for-everybody" bill. The southern states would get the most on a per capita basis, as shown in Table 5.16, which gives the per capita rankings for 1966-67.

TABLE 5.16

Estimated 1966–67 Distribution of Federal Grants Under the Canadian System to States in the United States Having Below-Average State-Local Revenue Capacity

State	Per Capita Amount	Amount (in millions)	Percentage of U.S. Total
South Carolina	$137	$356	7.7%
Mississippi	133	310	6.7
West Virginia	111	202	4.4
Alabama	110	388	8.4
Arkansas	102	201	4.3
North Carolina	95	473	10.2
Kentucky	89	282	6.1
Maine	83	82	1.8
Georgia	78	346	7.5
Tennessee	76	295	6.4
Virginia	72	324	7.0
Vermont	59	24	0.5
Pennsylvania	54	627	13.5
Rhode Island	43	39	0.8
Utah	43	43	0.9
Idaho	34	24	0.5
Missouri	29	131	2.8
South Dakota	19	13	0.3
Wisconsin	16	65	1.4
Texas	15	159	3.4
Ohio	12	122	2.6
Massachusetts	11	59	1.3
Indiana	9	43	0.9
Maryland	7	26	0.6
Minnesota	1	2	0.1

NOTE: These amounts are needed to make up the difference between the per capita state-local revenue capacity of each state and the nationwide per capita average for all state and local revenue sources.

SOURCE: ACIR, *Measuring the Fiscal Capacity and Effort of State and Local Areas* (Washington, D.C., 1971), p. 106.

Note the predominance of southern states in the list as might have been expected, only Florida and Louisiana being absent. There are also four New England states, Pennsylvania, and Ohio. The ranking of states in terms of the state-local grants of our 1972 federal assistance program makes an interesting comparison. Congress used the complex effort-plus-capacity formula described above, and the differences are significant (see Tables 5.16 and 5.17). Since the southern states in general have lower per capita income, the Canadian formula applied to our economy would mean more equitable distribution of federal revenues earmarked for sharing amongst the states.

Alternative Three:
Assumption of Functions

Another way to lighten city tax burdens is for higher level governments to assume entire responsibility for certain functions, paying for and administering these services themselves. Though the costs may be about the same, the two methods have administrative differences. Under the grants approach, the cities retain managerial autonomy. They may hire the people who administer the programs and tailor some of the rules to suit local conditions. Under the assumption-of-function approach, the administering bureaucracy is out of the control of the local political machine, an advantage or disadvantage, depending on one's point of view. State-wide or nationwide standards can be set to achieve desired uniformity more readily than with strings-attached categorical aids.

At the lowest level we find the frequent administration of welfare programs by counties for cities and other subcounty units. County financing, however, is only partial in most cases, substantial amounts of money being received from above. States administer unemployment insurance and placement programs in cities, but money for this is first collected by Washington from employers within the state and then returned to it except for a small percent-

TABLE 5.17

Ranking of Top 26 States by Amount of State-Local Grants Under 1972 U.S. General Revenue Sharing

State	Per Capita Grant
Mississippi	$40.9
South Dakota	38.0
Alabama	34.1
Vermont	33.6
New Mexico	32.8
New York	32.4
North Dakota	32.2
South Carolina	31.4
Washington, D.C.	31.4
Louisiana	31.2
Wisconsin	30.3
Hawaii	30.1
West Virginia	30.0
Utah	29.9
Montana	29.8
Wyoming	29.3
Delaware	29.2
Nebraska	28.9
Massachusetts	28.7
Arkansas	28.6
Arizona	28.3
Idaho	28.0
California	27.9
Iowa	27.3
Maryland	27.3
Georgia	23.8
States at the Bottom of the List	
Florida	21.5
Alaska	21.0
New Hampshire	20.8
Indiana	20.1
Ohio	19.4

SOURCE: Tabulated from Table I in ACIR, *Information Bulletin 72–8*, October 19, 1972, where Washington, D.C., is listed as though it were a state.

age that is retained for federal administrative costs. Medicare and Old Age and Survivors Annuities are two federal programs in which civil service employees in our cities are in national employ, not local.

Some city functions like health care are of the type that could easily be taken over by the federal government if put on an insurance-reimbursement basis, but direct ministration to the sick by clinics and hospitals would seem better left in local hands, either city or county. Regular financial aid to the blind or disabled is also appropriately a federal function. If the country were to move toward a negative income tax program for aid to the poor, this much of the welfare function could be shifted upward both in administration and in financing. If it remains on a means test basis requiring certification by case workers, financing may come from higher up, but administration should probably be left down where it is now.

The appropriateness of this method of solving the fiscal problems of our cities clearly depends on how much it adds to the intergovernmental grants approach. The 1972 adoption of federal general revenue sharing constituted a clear vote in favor of maintaining maximum local autonomy. Let Uncle Sam pay, but let cities administer their share.

Alternative Four:
Forming Larger Governmental Units to Aid Weaker Ones

When cities lose their upper income residents and businesses to their suburbs, an obvious remedy would be to redraw political boundaries to include these suburbs or even the whole metropolitan area within the same tax-paying political entity. This seems particularly logical when industrial city and residential suburbs are a close economic unit. It would permit spreading the costs over a broader tax base, reducing taxes in central cities while raising them outside. In its economic effects, this political consolidation is akin to what occurs when the state draws upon all of its taxpayers to provide help for cities in distress, causing higher taxes outside to permit lower taxes inside.

The difficulty with merging as a solution to urban fiscal difficulties is that the lower-taxed outside communities do not want to sacrifice their privileged position. This includes full autonomy in determining levels of services rendered. When such proposals are put to a vote they are usually defeated, and it is this prospect that causes cities to seek the more feasible alternative of getting state or federal help. This means spreading urban costs much more thinly per taxpayer and hence arouses less opposition. Most of what protest there may be can be overcome by vote trading or logrolling methods, which work sometimes in legislatures but rarely in annexation or consolidation elections.

Special districts that overlap independent jurisdictions are frequently formed for particular functions, however, like water supply, sewage disposal, drainage, flood control, bridge and tunnel building, and the like. There may be one big city and a lot of small ones in such districts, but general awareness of mutual problems brings them together. This is quite different from a central city asking that outlying communities bail it out.

Alternative Five:
  Cutting Expenses When Funds Are Insufficient

Whenever cities cannot raise enough money either internally or externally to pay budgeted amounts, they obviously will have to cut back somewhere. If it is necessary to prune expanding budgets, then citizens denied expected services will be disappointed. If existing budgets must be reduced, then employees will have to be laid off and item purchases curtailed. Reducing wage rates to distribute the retrenchment sacrifice more evenly among employees sometimes occurs in industry, but has rarely, if ever, been volunteered or negotiated with public workers.

Stories of school district financial difficulties are not uncommon. Schools have had to be closed for a month or more at a time to cut payroll expenses. In such cases, teachers and administrative and maintenance staffs, not to mention pupils, bear the brunt to save the taxpayers who have refused to vote the necessary funds. In city situations, whole departments are sometimes cut out or certain functions eliminated. At other times there is simply a freeze on new hiring, with attrition doing the payroll shrinking. Occasionally there are across-the-board cuts, with every department required to reduce its budget by, say, 5 or 10 percent.

According to a recent article by John Pazour, a not inconsiderable amount of curtailment has been going on. His summary table, reproduced as Table 5.18, indicates functions that have felt the ax but gives us no quantitative measurement of the dollars saved either in absolute amounts or as a percentage of budgets. We must also realize that the "savings" of one year's prunings may not persist. The next year's growth when more money has been found may exceed the prior pruning, as with many a growing tree. Only a very unlikely large and persistent decline in urban population would enable cities to make permanent budget cuts. Meanwhile, the demand for the urban services shows no sign of decline.

Perhaps more important than cutting expenses for most cities is firmer resistance to their increase. This is not easy because particular beneficiary groups see their own aggrandizement demands as urgent, fair, and for the public good. At the same time they see the cost of their increment as a very small portion of the total budget and therefore easily borne. Pay increases for various groups of employees, for instance; improvements in pensions, health insurance, and other fringe benefits; better facilities; and larger staffs, are a few illustrations. If a city were to cut its rate of annual expenditure increase by one-quarter, as from 12 percent to 9 percent, the likelihood of future budget crises would be substantially decreased. How to do this is a more difficult question. Courageous local leadership and continuing educational campaigns will be necessary, which is still a vague answer.

In private business, costs are reduced by increasing productivity in various ways, many of which the managers of government departments might emulate. Cities need research and develop-

TABLE 5.18

City Services and Capital Improvements Reduced Since 1963

Capital Improvements	Total	Reason for Reduction					
		Lack of Funds		Bonding Problems		Tax Restraints	
		Number of Cases	Percentage of Total	Number of Cases	Percentage of Total	Number of Cases	Percentage of Total
Expressways	20	9	45%	0	0%	11	55%
Street construction and maintenance	70	60	86	8	11	2	3
Lighting, traffic control	15	14	93	1	7	0	0
Urban renewal	6	4	67	0	0	2	33
Expansion of facilities	49	41	84	6	12	2	4
Water and sewers	70	67	96	3	4	0	0
Parks and recreation	87	76	87	8	9	3	3
Police (legal system)	56	51	91	4	7	1	2
Fire	59	55	93	3	5	1	2
Libraries	24	17	71	4	17	3	13
City government services	47	47	100	0	0	0	0

NOTE: 193 cities reporting.

SOURCE: John Pazour, "Local Government Fiscal Conditions," in International City Management Association, The Municipal Yearbook (Washington, D.C., 1972), p. 285.

ment programs to devise ways of improving the output per worker. In industry this is called innovation, technological progress. Cities do not need to invent new products; there is always a surfeit of them to be resisted, not added. But they do need labor-saving methods that prune staff deadwood, something public bureaucracies seem to accumulate more rapidly than private. Industry is very aware of the morale problem, how to get better performance from its workers. Governments should borrow some of their techniques—incentive payments, more interesting jobs, financial rewards for labor saving suggestions. Maybe deals could be worked out with unions representing public employees to enlist their help.

Confronted with serious budget problems some cities like New York have attempted to raise the productivity of city employees.[40] This involves the setting of measurable targets for specific tasks department by department and providing methods and incentives for their achievement. Mayor Lindsay, for instance, reported in January 1973, that goals established in early 1972 had been 77 percent achieved in the last six months of that year. "Of the 279 productivity targets, the report said, 152 were exceeded, 62 were met and 65 were 'missed.' In more than half of those missed, however, . . . performance still improved over the last year, for an over-all improvement level of 85 percent." Though widely present in well-managed business firms, this type of planning and achievement is too often lacking in government. Strong and imaginative leadership can do much to overcome entrenched laxities, managerial nonconcern, and union opposition.

Alternative Six:
Borrowing to Meet Revenue Deficits

Borrowing is only a temporary solution for city fiscal troubles, if even that. It may provide needed cash toward the end of a fiscal year, but only if two conditions are met: (1) there are no state limitations upon city borrowing, and (2) lenders can be found to buy the proffered notes or bonds. State laws differ. Some set a limit on the amount of borrowing that a city can do. Others forbid borrowing for current expenses except for tax-anticipation notes, which are supposed to be paid off before the beginning of the next fiscal year. When restrictions like these cannot be met, cities have to ask state legislatures to pass special bills giving them the right to depart from the general rules.

The easiest place to borrow, of course, is from some internal fund, even though that merely postpones the pain of cutting spending or raising taxes. Banks want to be sure that borrowed money can be repaid on schedule and therefore look at both prospective expenditures and any ceilings that may exist on revenue sources. The former could be reduced by city action, as suggested in the preceding section, but the latter can be lifted only by legislative or judicial action. (We mention the latter because default judgments obtained by creditors usually may be satisfied by tax increases that would otherwise be illegal.)

TABLE 5.19

City Short-Term Debt As a Percentage of General Revenues, 1955–72
(In millions)

Year	Short-Term Debt	Total General Revenue	Short-Term Debt As a Percentage of General Revenue
1955	$ 671	$ 7,824	8.58%
1960	1,274	11,647	10.94
1965	2,582	15,884	16.26
1970	4,903	26,621	18.42
1972	6,678	34,937	19.11

SOURCE: U.S. Bureau of the Census, *City Government Finances*, for various years.

Table 5.19 shows that the total amount of short-term debt outstanding has doubled every five years since 1955. This indicates a much more rapid growth than occurred in total city revenues. In 1955, short-term debt was only 8.6 percent of tax revenues, but by

1972 it had risen to over 19 percent. This could be interpreted as a response to increasing fiscal difficulties causing a more frequent recourse to borrowing to make ends meet. At the same time one must realize that fiscal difficulties do not occur to aggregates, they occur only to individual cities, and at particular times. Concealed in these figures are periods of anguish for certain city administrations that got caught in the trap of cumulative annual deficits. Sometimes creditors have gone to court demanding payment, and bankruptcy receivers, in effect, have been appointed to channel revenue to satisfy these claims. At other times distraught city officials have asked the help of state commissions in untangling the snarled web of fiscal mismanagement. Loan defaults, though infrequent since the Depression thirties, are the end of the line.

Can Cities Survive?

The foregoing description and analysis show that the question should really be "How Can Cities Survive?" That they do survive, that they have survived many fiscal crises is clear. But cities are basically people, and people have their discontents. They are not satisfied with this or that aspect of their lives. One group of dissatisfactions centers around the political-economic-social-geographic entities we call cities.

The urban situations that people don't like and want to improve range all the way from too high taxes to too few services. Some people deplore this aspect, and some deplore that. The dissatisfied people range from the powerful to the impotent, from the wealthy and the incumbents to the poor and the leaders of the party out of power. At any moment each sees the survival of his city somewhat differently. Each seeks to improve a different facet of the situation. Struggling against opposition and inertia, each may wonder whether his city as he sees it can survive the apathy, the greed, the short-sightedness, the tax burdens, the neglect, the deprivation, the whatever, that are the particular objects of his despair.

So, too, the methods differ that people follow in trying to ensure the healthier survival of their city, healthier when measured by their value scales. A "solution" from one point of view may be seen as a serious problem from another. One man's meat is another man's poison. Therefore no universal prescription is possible.

The authors have tried to show that situations differ as well as goals and that all benefits have costs. Each concerned citizen should be aware of the manifold alternatives and, weighing each carefully, push that one which seems best in the long run for himself, for his group, for his city as he sees it. Then in the give and take of the political process, the pulls and pressures of contending forces, our cities will move from one crisis to another, continuing to survive while forever changing and being changed.

Notes

1 On a national average, property taxes remain the largest single source of tax revenues in our cities, but the figure is less than half of the total, 49% in 1970 and falling. This means that, though they may be quite unaware of it, city dwellers in most cities are hurt more by other taxes and charges taken as a whole than by their property taxes. Tenants pay their share of the cities' property tax collections through their monthly rent payments. Not being very conscious of the tax-shifting involved, they speak out more frequently against sales or income tax increases than against property tax boosts, though in the long run it may be the latter that hit them the harder.

2 Saul Alinsky, *Rules for Radicals: A Practical Primer for Realistic Radicals* (New York: Random House, 1971).

3 Joint Economic Committee, 90th Congress, 1st Session, *Revenue Sharing and Its Alternatives: What Future for Fiscal Federalism?* Vol. 3, July 1967, pp. 1233-34.

4 ACIR, *Federal-State Co-ordination of Personal Income Taxes* (Washington, D.C., 1965), pp. 45-46.

5 Joint Economic Committee, *Revenue Sharing, op. cit.,* p. 1276.

6 David G. Otto, *et al., Nixon, McGovern and the Federal Budget* (Washington, D.C., American Enterprise Institute, 1972), p. 22.

7 *Ibid.,* p. 25.

8 *Ibid.,* p. 26; and U.S. Senate Subcommittee on Intergovernmental Relations, *Preliminary Results of the November 1972 Survey on Federal Grant System* (Washington, D.C., mimeo, no date).

9 Tax Foundation, *Fiscal Outlook for State and Local Governments to 1975* (New York, 1966).

10 Tax Foundation, *The Financial Outlook for State-Local Government to 1980—A Summary* (New York, 1973), p. 11. For details of various federal, state, and local fiscal projections, read Joint Economic Committee, 90th Congress, 1st Session, *Revenue Sharing and Its Alternatives: What Future For Fiscal Federalism?* Vol. 3, July 1967.

11 Weaker national governments than ours may get foreign aid from fiscally stronger ones, and even the United States has sought help from the International Monetary Fund and foreign governments in times of balance-of-payments crises.

12 David T. Bazelon, *The Paper Economy* (New York: Random House, 1963).

13 See J. M. Buchanan and M. Flowers, "An Analytical Setting for a Taxpayers' Revolution," *Western Economic Journal*, December 1969, pp. 349-59; and *The New York Times*, November 12, 1972, p. 23.

14 ACIR, *State-Local Taxation and Industrial Location* (Washington, D.C. 1967), p. 68.

15 Dick Netzer, *Economics of the Property Tax* (Washington, D.C.: Brookings Institution, 1966), pp. 175-76.

16 Average deviation of assessment ratios from the median ratio, as a percentage of the median value.

17 Frederick L. Bird, *The General Property Tax*, quoted in Netzer, *op. cit.*, p. 173.

18 U.S. Bureau of the Census, *Trends in Assessed Valuations and Sales Ratios, 1956-66*, State and Local Governments Special Studies No. 54, quoted in ACIR, *State-Local Finances: Significant Features and Suggested Legislation*, 1972 ed., p. 243.

19 It might even be possible to raise some of these ratios from present levels by capitalizing on prevailing sentiment such as that against speculators in vacant land. Raising land value taxation is the spirit of the Single Taxers, who seek to shift all the tax burden from improvements to land to promote justice and economic growth. Such shifting, however, would not produce more revenue, the cities' main objective.

20 Calculated from Department of Audit and Control, New York State, *Special Report on Municipal Affairs*, March 29, 1967, Tables 1 and 3; and Paul Corusy, "Improved Property Tax Administration: Legislative Opportunities and Probabilities," in Arthur D. Lynn, ed., *The Property Tax and Its Administration* (Madison: University of Wisconsin Press, 1969), p. 68.

21 *Demetrio Rodriguez, et al. v. San Antonio Independent School District, et al.*, 280 F. Supp. 1973; and U.S. Supreme Court Reports, March 21, 1973; Lawyer's Edition, April 23, 1973. Also note the *Serrano* case in California.

22 *The Wall Street Journal*, November 14, 1973, p. 1.

23 *The New York Times*, December 15, 1972, p. 1.

24 Henry M. Levin, *An Analysis of the Economic Effects of the New York City Sales Tax* (Washington, D.C.: Brookings Institution, 1967), Reprint 127.

25 Computed from Tables 59 and 125 in the Tax Foundation's *Facts and*

Figures on Government Finance (New York, 1971).

26 *Direct* federal aid was less than 10% as great as state aid to local governments in 1969, though a big change occurred in 1972 with the passage of the large revenue-sharing bill, as will be explained below.

27 S. F. Johnson and Paul E. Junk, "Sources of Tax Revenues and Expenditures in Large U.S. Cities," *Quarterly Review of Economics and Business,* Vol. 10, Winter 1970, pp. 7-15.

28 Another alternative is to borrow. Johnson and Junk explicitly state that "City expenditures stimulated by grants are financed largely by increasing city debt when types of taxation are limited. . . ." *Ibid.,* p. 13.

29 ACIR, *Measuring the Fiscal Capacity and Effort of State and Local Areas* (Washington, D.C., 1971), p. 7.

30 The ACIR has made up a suggestion list of underutilized tax sources for individual states but, unfortunately, not for cities. See Table 25, "Revenue Potential from Underutilized Tax Classes for States, 1966-67," in *Ibid.,* p. 79.

31 Executive Office of the President, Office of Management and Budget, *The United States Budget in Brief, Fiscal Year 1974,* p. 55.

32 ACIR, *Information Bulletin 72-8,* October 19, 1972, p. 7.

33 *Ibid.*

34 Walter W. Heller, *New Dimensions of Political Economy,* (New York: W. W. Norton, 1967), Ch. 3, pp. 117-72.

35 American Enterprise Institute, *Revenue Sharing Bills* (Washington, D.C., 1972).

36 For details see Edward R. Fried, *et al., Setting National Priorities: The 1974 Budget* (Washington, D.C.: Brookings Institution, 1973), pp. 180-84 and 208-14.

37 ACIR, *Measuring the Fiscal Capacity, op. cit.,* pp. 105-06.

38 *Ibid.,* pp. 106-07.

39 Paradoxically, in the same year that the U.S. Congress approved the new largesse formula for grants to state and local governments, the administration and the people generally disapproved strongly a similar proposal for individuals. The latter would have started with a uniform grant to everyone ($1,000 per year) and then used a progressive income tax to take back an increasing fraction of it as personal incomes rose. The net would then be graduated according to need without requiring any complex formula to determine how much need existed.

40 *The New York Times,* February 16, 1972, and January 18, 1973.

BIBLIOGRAPHY

Advisory Commission on Intergovernmental Relations. *Alternative Approaches to Governmental Reorganization in Metropolitan Areas.* Washington, D.C. 1962.

———. *City Financial Emergencies: The Intergovernmental Dimension.* Washington, D.C. 1973.

———. *The Commuter and the Municipal Income Tax.* Washington, D.C. 1970.

———. *Fiscal Balance in the American Federal System,* Vol. 2, *Metropolitan Fiscal Disparities.* Washington, D.C. 1967.

———. *Governmental Structure and Planning in Metropolitan Areas.* Washington, D.C. 1961.

———. *Local Non-Property Taxes and the Coordinating Role of the State.* Washington, D.C. 1961.

———. *Measures of State and Local Fiscal Capacity and Tax Effort.* Washington, D.C. 1962.

———. *Measuring the Fiscal Capacity and Effort of State and Local Areas.* Washington, D.C. 1971.

———. *Metropolitan Social and Economic Disparities: Implications for Intergovernmental Relations in Central Cities and Suburbs.* Washington, D.C. 1965.

———. *Performance of Urban Functions: Local and Areawide.* Washington, D.C. 1963.

———. *The Role of Equalization in Federal Grants.* Washington, D.C. 1964.

———. *The Role of the States in Strengthening the Property Tax.* 2 volumes. Washington, D.C. 1963.

———. *State Aid to Local Governments.* Washington, D.C. 1969.

———. *State and Local Taxation of Privately Owned Property Located on Federal Areas.* Washington, D.C. 1961.

———. *State-Local Finances: Significant Features and Suggested Legislation, 1972.* Washington, D.C. 1972.

151

————. *State-Local Taxation and Industrial Location.* Washington, D.C. 1967.

————. *Urban America and the Federal System.* Washington, D.C. 1969.

————. *Urban and Rural America: Policies for Future Growth.* Washington, D.C. 1968.

Alinsky, Saul. *Rules for Radicals: A Practical Primer for Realistic Radicals.* New York. Random House. 1971.

American Enterprise Institute. *Nixon, McGovern and the Federal Budget.* Washington, D.C. 1972.

————. *Revenue Sharing Bills, An Analysis of Proposals to Share Federal Revenue with State and Local Governments.* Washington, D.C. 1972.

Bahl, Roy. *Metropolitan City Expenditures.* Lexington, Ky. University of Kentucky Press. 1969.

————. "Public Policy and the Urban Fiscal Problem: Piecemeal vs. Aggregate Solutions." *Land Economics.* Vol. 46, No. 1, Feb. 1970.

Banfield, Edward. *The Unheavenly City.* Boston. Little, Brown. 1970.

Baumol, William. "Macroeconomics of Unbalanced Growth: The Anatomy of Urban Crises." *American Economic Review.* June 1967.

Bazelon, David. *The Paper Economy.* New York. Random House. 1963.

Benson, George, *et al.* *The American Property Tax: Its History, Administration, and Economic Impact.* Claremont, Calif. Claremont Men's College. 1965.

Birch, David L. *The Economic Future of City and Suburb.* New York. Committee for Economic Development. 1970.

Bish, Robert. *The Public Economy of Metropolitan Areas.* Chicago. Markham Publishing Company. 1971.

Bollens, John, and Schmandt, Henry. *The Metropolis: Its People, Politics and Economic Life.* New York. Harper & Row. 1965.

Borcherding, T. E., and Deacon, R. T. "The Demand for the Services of Non-Federal Governments." *American Economic Review.* Dec. 1972.

Bradford, A. F., *et al.* "The Rising Cost of Local Public Services: Some Evidence and Reflections." *National Tax Journal.* Vol. 22, No. 2, June 1969.

Brazer, Harvey. *City Expenditures in the United States.* New York. National Bureau of Economic Research. 1959.

————. *Essays in State and Local Finance.* Ann Arbor, Mich. Institute of Public Administration, University of Michigan. 1967.

————. "Some Fiscal Implications of Metropolitanism." In Guthrie Birkhead, ed. *Metropolitan Issues: Social, Governmental, Fiscal.* Syracuse, N.Y. Maxwell Graduate School of Public Affairs of Syracuse University. 1962.

————, and Margolis, Julius. "Municipal Fiscal Structure in a Metropolitan Region." *Journal of Political Economy*. Vol. 55, June 1957.

Break, George. "Financing of Local Government," Sacramento, Calif. Advisory Commission on Tax Reform: Researcher's Tentative Report. Oct. 1968.

————. *Intergovernmental Fiscal Relations in the United States*. Washington, D.C. Brookings Institution. 1967.

Buchanan, J. M., and Flowers, M., "An Analytical Setting for a Taxpayers' Revolution." *Western Economic Journal*. Dec. 1969.

Bureau of Business Research. *America's Cities*. Ann Arbor, Mich. University of Michigan. 1970

Burkhead, Jesse. "Uniformity in Government Expenditures of Resources in a Metropolitan Area." *National Tax Journal*. Vol. 14, No. 4, Dec. 1961.

Campbell, Allen, ed. *The States and the Urban Crisis*. New York. Columbia University Press. 1970.

————. "Taxes and Industrial Location in the New York Metropolitan Region." *National Tax Journal*. Vol. 11, No. 3, Sept. 1958.

————. and Sacks, Seymour. *Metropolitan America: Fiscal Patterns and Government Systems*. New York. Free Press. 1967.

Chinitz, Benjamin, ed. *City and Suburbs*. Englewood Cliffs, N. J. Prentice-Hall. 1965.

Clark, Kenneth. *The Dark Ghetto*. New York. Harper & Row. 1965.

Cohen, Jerry, and Murphy, William. *Burn Baby Burn*. New York. Avon Books. 1966.

Committee for Economic Development. *Modernizing Local Government*. New York. 1966.

————. *Reshaping Government in Metropolitan Areas*. New York. 1970.

Conant, James. *Slums and Suburbs*. New York. McGraw Hill. 1961.

Conference Board. *Government Services in Major Metropolitan Areas*. New York. 1972.

Connery, Robert, ed. *Municipal Income Taxes*. New York. Academy of Political Sciences, Columbia University. 1968.

Crecine, John. *Financing the Metropolis: Public Policy In Urban Economics*. Urban Affairs Annual Reviews. Vol. 4. Beverly Hills, Calif. Sage Publications. 1970.

Crouch, Winston. "Conflict and Co-operation Among Local Governments in the Metropolis." *Annals of the American Academy of Political and Social Science*. Vol. 359, May 1965.

Davies, David. "Financing Urban Functions and Services." *Law and Contemporary Problems*. Vol. 30, No. 1, Winter 1965.

Davis, Otto, and Haines, George. "A Political Approach to a Theory of Public Expenditures: The Case of Municipalities." *National Tax Journal.* Vol. 19, No. 3, Sept. 1966.

Due, John. *State and Local Sales Taxation: Structure and Administration.* Chicago. Public Administration Services. 1971.

Duhl, Leonard, ed. *The Urban Condition.* New York. Basic Books. 1963.

Duncan, O. *Metropolis and Region.* Baltimore. Johns Hopkins Press. 1960.

Ecker-Racz, L. *The Politics and Economics of State-Local Finance.* Englewood Cliffs, N. J. Prentice-Hall. 1970.

Eels, R. ed. *Man in the City of the Future.* New York. McMillan. 1969.

Elison, Larry. *The Finances of Metropolitan Areas.* Ann Arbor, Mich. University of Michigan Law School. 1964.

Executive Office of the President, Office of Management and Budget. *The United States Budget in Brief, Fiscal Year 1974.* Washington, D.C., 1973.

Fabricant, Solomon. *The Trend of Government Activity in the United States Since 1900.* New York. National Bureau of Economic Research. 1952.

Fisher, Glenn. "Determinants of State and Local Government Expenditures: A Preliminary Analysis." *National Tax Journal.* Vol. 14 No. 4, Dec. 1961.

Forrester, Jay W. *Urban Dynamics.* Cambridge, Mass. Massachusetts Institute of Technology Press. 1969.

Fried, Edward R., *et al., Setting National Priorities: The 1974 Budget.* Washington, D.C. Brookings Institution. 1973.

Frieden, Beynard. *The Future of Old Neighborhoods.* Cambridge, Mass. Massachusetts Institute of Technology Press. 1964.

Ginger, Ray, ed. *Modern American Cities.* Chicago. Quadrangle Books. 1965.

Glaab, Charles. *The American City, A Documentary History.* Homewood, Ill. Dorsey Press. 1963.

————, and Brown, A. Theodore. *History of Urban America.* New York. Macmillan. 1967.

Glazer, Nathan, ed. *Cities in Trouble.* Chicago. Quadrangle Books. 1970.

————, and McEntire, Davis, eds. *Studies in Housing and Minority Groups.* Berkeley. University of California Press. 1960.

Glazer, Sidney. *Detroit: A Study in Urban Development.* New York. Twayne. 1965.

Green, Constance. *The Rise of Urban America.* New York. Harper & Row. 1965.

Green, Scott. *Urban Renewal and American Cities.* Indianapolis. Bobbs-Merrill. 1965.

Groves, Harold. *Financing Government.* New York. Holt, Rinehart and Winston. 1964.

Hadden, Jeffrey, *et al. Metropolis in Crisis.* Itasca, Ill. F. E. Peacock Publishers. 1967.

Hansen, Niles. "The Structure and Determinants of Local Public Investment Expenditure." *Review of Economics and Statistics.* Vol. 47, No. 2, May 1965.

Harriss, Lowell, *Handbook of State and Local Government Finance.* New York. Tax Foundation. 1966.

Hartman, Paul. *Wage Effects of Local Government Employees Bargaining.* Bureau of National Affairs. May 10, 1971.

Hatt, Paul, and Reiss, Albert, eds. *Cities and Society.* New York. Free Press. 1957.

Hauser, Philip, and Schnore, Leo. *The Study of Urbanization.* New York. John Wiley. 1965.

Hawley, Amos. "Metropolitan Population and Municipal Government Expenditures in Central Cities." *Review of Economics and Statistics.* Vol. 47, No. 2, May 1965.

Haworth, Lawrence. *The Good City.* Bloomington, Ind. Indiana University Press. 1963.

Heilbrun, James. *Real Estate Taxes and Urban Housing.* New York. Columbia University Press. 1966.

―――. *Urban Economics and Public Policy.* New York. St. Martin's Press. 1973.

Heller, Walter. *New Dimensions of Political Economy.* New York. W. W. Norton. 1967.

Hempel, George. *The Postwar Quality of State and Local Debt.* National Bureau of Economic Research. General Series, No. 54. New York. Columbia University Press. 1971.

Hirsch, Werner. *The Economics of State and Local Government.* New York. McGraw-Hill. 1970.

―――. "Expenditure of Metropolitan Growth and Consolidation." *Review of Economics and Statistics.* Vol. 41, No. 3, Aug. 1959.

―――. *Measuring Factors Affecting Expenditure Levels for Local Government Services.* St. Louis. Metropolitan State University Survey. 1957.

―――. *A Statistical Sketch of State and Local Government Activities.* Los Angeles. University of California, Institute of Government and Public Affairs. 1967.

————. *Urban Economic Analysis*. New York. McGraw-Hill. 1973.

————, et al. *Fiscal Pressures on the Central City*. New York. Praeger. 1971.

Hodge, Patricia, and Hauser, Philip. *The Challenge of America's Metropolitan Population Outlook, 1960-1985*. (Research Report, No. 3.) Washington, D.C. National Commission on Urban Problems. 1968.

Holland, Daniel, ed. *The Assessment of Land Values*. Madison, Wis. University of Wisconsin Press. 1970.

Hoover, Edgar and Vernon, R. *Anatomy of a Metropolis*. Cambridge, Mass. Harvard University Press. 1959.

International City Management Association. *The Municipal Yearbook*. Washington, D.C. 1972.

Isard, Walter, and Coughlin, Robert. *Municipal Costs and Revenues*. Wellesley, Mass. Chandler-Davis. 1957.

Jacobs, Jane. *The Death and Life of Great American Cities*. New York. Random House. 1961.

————. *The Economy of Cities*. New York. Random House. 1969.

Johnson, S., and Junk, P. "Sources of Tax Revenues and Expenditures in Large United States Cities." *Quarterly Review of Economics and Business*. Vol. 10, Winter 1970.

Kaun, D., and Spiro, M. "The Relation Between Wages and Unemployment in United States Cities, 1955-1965." *Manchester School of Economic and Social Studies*. Vol. 38, March 1970.

Kee, Woo Sik. "Central City Expenditures and Metropolitan Areas." *National Tax Journal*. Vol. 18, No. 4, Dec. 1965.

————. "City-Suburban Differentials in Local Government: Fiscal Effects." *National Tax Journal*. Vol. 21, No. 2, June 1968.

Kurnow, Ernest. "Determinants of State and Local Expenditures Reexamined." *National Tax Journal*. Vol. 16, No. 3, Sept. 1963.

Leahy, William, et al. *Urban Economics*. New York. Free Press. 1970.

Levin, Henry M. *An Analysis of the Economic Effects of the New York City Sales Tax*. Washington, D.C. Brookings Institute. 1967.

Levin, Melvin R., ed. *Exploring Urban Problems*. Boston. Urban Press. 1971.

Levy, Michael E., and de Torres, Juan. *Federal Revenue Sharing with the States, Problems and Promises*. New York. National Industrial Conference Board. 1970.

Lichtenberg, Robert. *One-Tenth of a Nation*. Cambridge, Mass. Harvard University Press. 1960.

Lindsay, John. *The City*. New York. New American Library. 1970.

Lockard, Duane. *The Politics of State and Local Government.* New York. Macmillan. 1963.

Lynn, Arthur. *The Property Tax and its Administration.* Madison, Wis. University of Wisconsin Press. 1969.

McCord, William. *Life Style in the Black Ghetto.* New York. W. W. Norton. 1969.

McKean, Roland. *Public Spending.* New York. McGraw-Hill. 1968.

McKelvey, Blake. *The Urbanization of America.* New Brunswick, N.J. Rutgers University Press. 1962.

Maier, Henry. *Challenge of the Cities.* New York. Random House. 1966.

Margolis, Julius. "Municipal Fiscal Structure in a Metropolitan Region." *Journal of Political Economy.* Vol. 65, No. 3, June 1957.

————, ed. *The Public Economy of Urban Communities.* Baltimore. Johns Hopkins Press. 1965.

Martin, Roscoe, *The Cities and the Federal System.* New York. Atherton. 1965.

Maxwell, James. *Financing State and Local Government.* Washington, D.C. Brookings Institution. 1965.

Mikesell, John. "Central Cities and Sales Tax Differentials." *National Tax Journal.* Vol. 3, No. 2, June 1970.

Mitchell, Gordon. *Sick Cities.* Baltimore. Penguin Books. 1967.

Mumford, Lewis. *The Highway and the City.* New York. New American Library. 1964.

Muskin, Selma, and Cotton, Joseph F. *Functional Federalism.* Washington, D.C. State and Local Finances Project of the George Washington University. 1968.

————, ————. *Sharing Federal Funds for State and Local Needs.* New York. Praeger. 1969.

Neenan, William. "Suburban-Central City Exploitation Thesis: One City's Tales." *National Tax Journal.* Vol. 23, No. 2, June 1970.

Netzer, Dick. *Economics and Urban Problems.* New York. Basic Books. 1970.

————. *Economics of the Property Tax.* Washington, D.C. Brookings Institution. 1966.

————. "Financial Needs and Resources Over the Next Decade: State and Local Government." *Public Finances: Needs, Sources, and Utilization.* Princeton. National Bureau of Economic Research. 1961.

————, ed. *Financing Government in New York City.* New York. 1966.

————. *Impact of the Property Tax: Its Economic Implications for Urban Problems,* Washington, D.C. Joint Economic Committee of U.S. Congress. 1968.

New York State Department of Audit and Control. *Special Report on Municipal Affairs.* Albany. 1967.

Osofsky, Gilbert. *Harlem, The Making of a Ghetto.* New York. Harper & Row. 1963.

Pechman, Joseph A. *Federal Tax Policy.* revised edition. New York. W. W. Norton. 1971.

Perloff, Harvey, and Richard, Nathan, eds. *Revenue Sharing and the City.* Baltimore. Johns Hopkins Press. 1968.

————, and Wingo, Lowdon, eds. *Issues in Urban Economics.* Baltimore. Johns Hopkins Press. 1968.

Pettengill, Robert B., Uppal, J. S., and Chen, Kuan-I. *Cities and Suburbs —The Case for Equity.* Albany, N.Y. New York Conference of Mayors and Municipal Officials. 1970.

Pidot, George. "A Principal Components Analysis of the Determinants of Local Government Fiscal Patterns." *Review of Economics and Statistics.* Vol. 6, No. 2, May 1969.

————. "The Public Finances of Metropolitan Government in the Metropolitan United States." (Doctoral dissertation.) Cambridge, Mass. Harvard. 1966.

Reissman, Leonard. *The Urban Process, Cities in Industrial Societies.* New York. Free Press. 1964.

Renshaw, E. F. "State and Local Government Surpluses in Budgets—Are They Fact or Fiction?" *Money Manager.* No. 20, November 20, 1972.

Sacks, Seymour, and Harris, Robert. "The Determinants of State and Local Government Expenditures and Intergovernmental Flow of Funds." *National Tax Journal.* Vol. 17, No. 1, March 1964.

Sacks, Seymour, *et al. Financing Government in a Metropolitan Area: The Cleveland Experience.* Glencoe, Ill.: Free-Press. 1971.

Sales Management, Editors of. "Survey of Buying Power." *Sales Management.* June or July, annually.

Schaller, Howard, *Public Expenditure Decisions in the Urban Community.* Baltimore. Johns Hopkins Press. 1963.

Schmandt, Henry J., and Stephens, Ross. "Local Government Expenditure Patterns in the United States." *Land Economics.* Vol. 39, No. 4, Nov. 1963.

Schnore, Leo. *The Urban Scene.* New York. Free Press. 1965.

Schultze, Charles, *et al.* "Fiscal Problems of Cities." *Setting National Priorities: The 1973 Budget.* Washington, D.C. Brookings Institution. 1972.

Scott, Claudia D. *Forecasting Local Government Spending.* Washington, D.C. Urban Institute. 1972.

Scott, Stanley, and Feder, Edward. *Factors Associated with Variations in Municipal Expenditure Levels.* Berkeley. University of California, Bureau of Public Administration. 1957.

Shapiro, Harvey. "Economies of Scale and Local Government Finance." *Land Economics.* Vol. 39, No. 2, May 1963.

Sherman, Richard. *The Negro and the City.* Englewood Cliffs, N.J. Prentice-Hall. 1970.

Smith, Wade. "Municipal Financing in the 1970's." (Unpublished paper presented to the 29th annual conference of the Municipal Finance Officers Association.) Denver, Colo. April 20, 1971.

Sofen, Edward. *Miami Metropolitan Experiment.* Bloomington, Ind. Indiana University Press. 1963.

Stanley, David. *Managing Local Governments Under Pressure.* Washington, D.C. Brookings Institution. 1972.

Starr, Roger, *Urban Choices.* Baltimore. Penguin Books. 1967.

Stephens, G. Ross, and Schmandt, Henry. "Revenue Patterns of Local Governments." *National Tax Journal.* Vol. 15, No. 4, Dec. 1962.

Tax Foundation, Inc. *Big City Revenue Structures in Transition.* New York. 1972.

————. *Facts and Figures on Government Finance.* 17th edition. New York. 1972.

————. *Federal Grants: The Need for Reform.* New York. 1973.

————. *Federal Revenue Sharing.* New York. 1970.

————. *Fiscal Outlook for State and Local Government to 1975.* New York. 1966.

————. *Non-Tax Revenues.* New York. 1968.

————. *Projections of State-Local Finances to 1980.* New York. 1972.

————. *State and Local Sales Taxes.* New York. 1970.

Teeples, Ronald. *Some Problems Concerning the Magnitude of State and Local Government Revenues From User Charges.* Los Angeles. University of California, Institute of Government and Public Affairs. 1968.

Thompson, Wilbur. *A Preface to Urban Economics.* Baltimore. Johns Hopkins Press. 1965.

Tiebout, Charles. "A Pure Theory of Local Expenditures." *Journal of Political Economy.* Vol. 64, Oct. 1965.

U.S. Congress, House of Representatives, Committee on Ways and Means. *Hearings on General Revenue Sharing.* June 1971.

U.S. Congress, Joint Economic Committee. *Revenue Sharing and Its Alternatives: What Future For Fiscal Federalism?* Vols. I, II, and III. 1967.

————. *State and Local Facility Needs and Financing.* Vol. I. *Public Facility Needs.* 1966.

U.S. Congress, Senate Select Committee on Nutrition and Human Needs. *Hunger 1973.* Washington, D.C. 1973.

U.S. Congress, Senate Subcommittee on Intergovernmental Relations. *Preliminary Results of the November 1972 Survey on Federal Grant System.* Washington, D.C. No date.

U.S. Department of Commerce, Bureau of the Census. *Census of Governments, 1967: State Payments to Local Governments.* Washington, D.C. 1968.

————. *Census of Governments: Property Tax Rates in Selected Major Cities and Counties.* 1968.

————. *Census of Governments: Taxable Property Values.* 1962 and 1966.

————. *City Government Finances.* 1950-72.

———— *General Demographic Trends for Metropolitan Areas 1960-1970.* 1972.

————. *Governmental Finances.* 1967-72.

————. *Historical Statistics on State and Local Government Finances, 1902-1953.* Special Studies, No. 38. 1955.

————. *Local Government Finances in Selected Metropolitan Areas.* 1950-70.

————. *State Government Finances.* 1950-70.

————. *Statistical Abstract of the United States.* 1950-72.

————. *Trends in Social and Economic Conditions in Metropolitan and Non-Metropolitan Areas.* Special Studies, No. 33. 1970.

U.S. Federal Bureau of Investigation. *Uniform Crime Reports for the United States.* 1970.

Vernon, Raymond. *The Changing Economic Function of the Central City.* New York. Committee for Economic Development. 1969.

————. *Metropolis, 1985.* New York. Anchor Books. 1963.

————. *The Myth and Reality of Our Urban Problems.* Cambridge, Mass. Harvard University Press. 1966.

Vietorisz, Harrison. *Economic Development of Harlem, 1970.* New York. Praeger. 1970.

Walker, Mabel. *Urban Blight and Slums.* Cambridge, Mass. Harvard University Press. 1938.

Warner, Sam. *Streetcar Suburbs.* Cambridge, Mass. Harvard University Press. 1962.

Weaver, Robert. *Dilemmas of Urban America.* Cambridge, Mass. Harvard University Press. 1967.

Weicher, J. "Determinants of Central City Expenditures, Some Overlooked Factors and Problems." *National Tax Journal*. Vol. 23, No. 4, Dec. 1970.

Weintraub, Robert. *Options for Meeting the Revenue Needs of City Governments*. Santa Barbara, Calif. Tempo, General Electric. 1967.

Wheaton, William, *et al*. *Urban Housing*. New York. Free Press. 1966.

Williams, Oliver, *et al*. *Suburban Differences and Metropolitan Policies: A Philadelphia Story*. Pittsburgh. University of Pennsylvania Press. 1965.

Wilson, James, ed. *The Metropolitan Enigma*. Cambridge, Mass. Harvard University Press. 1968.

————. *Urban Renewal: The Record and the Controversy*. Cambridge, Mass. Massachusetts Institute of Technology Press 1967.

Wood, Robert. *Fourteen Hundred Governments*. Cambridge, Mass. Harvard University Press. 1961.

Woodbury, Coleman, ed. *The Future of Cities and Urban Redevelopment*. Chicago. University of Chicago Press. 1953.

Wright, Frank Lloyd. *The Living City*. New York. Horizon. 1958.

INDEX

Intergovernmental aid *(continued)*
centage of total city budget, 49, 50;
as a rational choice, 114-139; substitutive and stimulative, 52-55;
variations in, 55, 72; *see also*
General Revenue Sharing, Special
Revenue Sharing
Interregional competition, 94

Jacobs, Jane, 6, 57, 83
Jersey City, 57
Johnson, S. F., 149
Joint Economic Committee, U.S.
Congress, 56, 87, 148
Junk, Paul, 149

Kansas City, 47, 77
Kee, Woo, 77, 84

Levin, Henry, 149
Licenses, 49
Lindsay, John, 7, 145
Long Beach, revenue-raising capacity
of, 125
Los Angeles, 39, 65, 70, 75, 80
Lupo, G., 87
Lynn, Arthur, 149

Mikesell, John L., 46, 56
Mushkin, S., 87

National League of Cities, 87
Negative income tax, 141
Netzer, Dick, 33, 87, 106, 149
Newark, 65, 70, 77, 114, 116
New Orleans, 77, 131
New York City, 65, 72, 75, 80, 111,
114, 116, 129, 131
New York State, revenue-sharing al-
lotment for, 129
New York Times, 82, 149, 150
Nixon budget, 89, 136
Nonproperty taxes, 41-49; *see also*
Income tax, Sales tax
Nonwhites: as cause of city spend-
ing, 20; educational expenses for,
24; enrollment of, in public
schools, 24; fiscal impact of, 22-
30; percentage of, in central cities,
24, 60; in suburbs, 60; welfare
expenses for, 24

Overlapping jurisdictions: and fiscal
capacity, 125; and statistics, 11-12

Packard, Vance, 115
Parochial schools, 90
Paterson (N.J.), 70
Pazour, John, 33, 56, 143, 144
Pentagon, 134
Personalty, taxing of, 105
Pettengill, Robert, 84
Philadelphia, 41, 75
Phoenix, noneducational expenditures
in, 65
Pittsburgh, revenue-sharing funds in
budget of, 131
Plato, 85
Police expenditures, 16, 27-29
"Poor" cities in the U.S., 123, 124
Population changes, 15, 22, 32
Population density, 22, 23, 27
Portland, property tax base in, 80
Poverty: as cause of city spending,
20; and fiscal effort, 116; and in-
tergovernmental aid, 116
Power groups, 86
Private schools, 67
Productivity, 17, 145
Property tax, 36-40, 86, 95-111; on
commercial and residential income
property, 101; dependence on, 39;
difficulties in raising, 95; exemptions from, 108-109; general, 37-
40; increase of, in selected cities,
40; and mortgage payments, 99;
protest against, 99; reform of, 105-
109; on regulated monopolies,
100; relief from, 4, 109-111; resistance to, 100; and school financing, 99, 109-110; shifting of, to
customers and tenants, 100-101;
tax roll for, 108
Providence (R.I.), tax burden in, 77

Real estate, market value of, 122
Reassessment, piecemeal, 103
Resort cities, 13, 27-28
Retail sales tax, *see* Sales tax
Revenues, city, 35-56; capacity vs.
effort, 125-126; compared to ex-
penditures, 35, 87; deficiencies of,